Genealogical Jaunts

Travels in Family History

by

Dennis Ford

Genealogical Jaunts
Travels in Family History

iUniverse books may be ordered through booksellers or by contacting:

iUniverse
1663 Liberty Drive
Bloomington, IN 47403
www.iuniverse.com
844-349-9409

ISBN: 978-1-4401-0685-9 (sc)
ISBN: 978-1-4401-3781-5 (hc)
ISBN: 978-1-4401-0686-6 (e)

Print information available on the last page.

iUniverse rev. date: 10/28/2020

To my fellow travelers

These eight chapters represent eight journeys made on behalf of history and family history—they are eight among many more journeys that remain undocumented. The journeys were made in the time period 1996-2007. I was accompanied by Sophia Ford, who became a world traveler in her senior years. In these pages she is referred to as "Babci", which is Polish for "grandmother". Babci is a word that replaced her personal name since the birth of her first grandchild in 1975. She's rarely been called anything else since. On several of these journeys we were accompanied by additional family members—on one trip eight relatives traveled with us.

The chapters are based on copious notes I made each evening of our journeys. I dutifully recorded my memories of the day's events, the places we visited, the people we met. These recollections are as accurate as anything—I trust paper and pen more than I trust neurons and glia. I may have forgotten events, but I was careful not to make any up. I also incorporated factual details available in pamphlets and guidebooks—we have to trust the authors of these books didn't make anything up. When we returned to the States I organized my notes and wrote travel essays under the chapter headings in this book. The essays were photocopied and distributed among family and friends.

Last year I became motivated to create a book of essays that had laid in folders, some for as long as a decade. I tried not to add or to edit anything—I trust memory less as the years roll by. There have been changes, of course, in the flow of events—Danislav Storta and Juzufa Kozlowska have died, Dauphin Island was rolled over by a storm, and hurricanes nearly destroyed New Orleans, Pensacola, and Biloxi—but I didn't update anything or perform additional research. Nor did I edit for redundancy. Each essay was left essentially as written in the year of the journey described.

A wise person once observed that one of the ideals of the good life is to experience pleasant thoughts in the moments of solitude. I am a most fortunate person in that regard. In my moments of solitude I often think of the journeys described in *Genealogical Jaunts*. At such moments I feel a deep sense of gratitude and a connectedness with family and with the history we've encountered pursuing our ancestry. I've traversed the world from Pensacola to Palanga—doing so, I've managed to find home.

THE AMBER COUNTRY

Lithuania—June, 1997

Kalniskes

We visited Kalniskes, the ancestral village of the Bielawski family, on June 7. Our translator was Irena B—, a short middle-aged lady. Our driver was a young man named Kestas. The trip from the Hotel Naujasis Vilnius, where we were staying, took approximately thirty-five minutes. The roads were in good condition until we reached Turgeli, the parish town that demarcated less primitive from more primitive. The final portion of the trip was made by cutting across pasture.

A stretch of road a few miles south of Vilnius was especially picturesque. The road runs between rows of very tall and aged trees and gives the impression that the vehicle is approaching a country house through an arboreal tunnel. Irena informed us that such roads were common before everything fell apart under communism.

I recorded the following observations as we drove south of Turgeli. We passed cars, but we also passed several horse-drawn wagons. No tractors were observed, or none of any size. Several farmers worked their fields using horses. Also, farmers were observed cutting grass with a large tool that resembled a scythe. Some of the farmers—the ones bending down—were women dressed

1

in stereotypical Slavic regalia of babushkas, full-length skirts, and long-sleeved blouses. There didn't appear to be much cultivation of crops in the fields we drove by. The only cultivation we saw were small gardens close to farmhouses. Probably, the majority of land is used for pasture, as it was mostly grass and cows reclined in the fields alongside the road.

There wasn't a centrally organized village (*kaimas*) of Kalniskes. Rather, there were a few farms spread out in what looked to be haphazard fashion. The land is very green and grassy, with a few gentle hills in sight. (The word *Kalniskes* means "hill" in Lithuanian.) The Bielawski farm was situated in a wooded swale. As we cut across the field, the roofs of the farmhouse and barn were visible but nothing of their walls. The trees and the sunken position of the buildings provide shelter from what must be severe winters.

Michail Bielawski is Babci's first cousin. He is a short man of slight build, with a reddish face and small blue eyes. His hair is mostly gray and cropped close in a crew-cut. He is fifty-seven years old. He has the characteristic Bielawski nose and somewhat resembles my grandfather Paul around the eyes. Babci thinks he resembles his uncle Josef.

Helena Dashevic is his wife. Helena is a tiny person, not five feet tall. She has a red face and prominent front teeth. She is an emotional and energetic lady. She does a lot of the farm work, including gardening and managing the pigs.

Their sons are Mecislav and Viktor. Both are short and slim of build. Mecislav, who is twenty five, has a receding hairline; his hair is blond. His eyes are closely spaced and there's a look of worry fixed on his face. He works in "technics", which means auto mechanics.

Viktor is eighteen. He is taller than his brother and has longer blond hair. He has prominent teeth like Helena and a somewhat long aspect to his face. His hands are workman's hands, large and heavily muscled.

The Bielawski farm is situated as follows. The land near the entrance to the property is yellow soil, clear of grass. A stack of hay is on the left side of the path and, closer to the house, there's a huge pile of wood. A work shed is between the haystack and the woodpile. The opening to the shed is quite wide, but it was dark inside and we couldn't see what it was used for. To the right of the woodpile is a small coop or pen. No animals were inside. The house is a small, single-story wood structure painted bright blue. A large barn is across from the house. The land behind the house and to the left—the direction from which we approached—is pasture. The land in front of the house and to the right is heavily wooded. In the woods a cow stands tethered to a tree.

We took the Bielawski family by surprise, as they had not received our letter. Michail was working near the barn, Viktor in the shed. Both had dirty hands and were sweating profusely. We waited outside the house while

Helena hurried inside to clean up. With the assistance of Irena we made small talk with various members of the family while the others changed into their Sunday finery.

Helena went on motorbike to a local store to purchase soda and liquor. One bottle was a locally-brewed vodka. Another was a liquor called Daiwana that tasted like brandy, but was not as high in proof. I don't know where the local store was. I observed a tiny store near the church in Turgeli, but that seemed a considerable distance to go.

When she returned, Helena put out quite a spread in our honor. Besides the liquor, there were several kinds of meat, sliced cucumbers and tomatoes, dark bread, and pickles. For some reason Michail was very proud of the pickles. I'm not sure why he was so proud—a pickle is just a cucumber on Social Security. In addition, there were several varieties of wrapped candies. The ones I sampled had a coconut flavor.

The entrance to their home was on the left side of the building. The kitchen was directly ahead. We were entertained in the parlor, which was on the right. This room ran the entire front side of the house. A curtain and three large cabinets separated it from the rest of the interior—my guess is the curtains hid a bedroom. A table was near the right corner of the parlor. A low couch stood beneath windows that opened to the front. A stool with a rather large plant was beneath a window on the adjacent wall. This plant resembled a kind of vine or cactus. Irena explained that it kept flies away and was believed to have medicinal powers. Several framed pictures of the Blessed Mother hung in the corner between windows. I did not see any family photographs.

Michail explained that he worked as a driver on a collective farm for thirty years. He is deeply upset because his pension will cover only the last seven years—the years since Lithuanian independence. He spoke quite bitterly about this, calling his pension records "worthless".

He is out of steady work with the elimination of collective farming. The farm is basically one of sustenance—producing just enough to feed his family and make a little money. On the farm they have three pigs, three cows, a horse, and numerous chickens. There are several cats as well, one of which pestered us for scraps.

He is angry about the government, feeling that it betrayed the working class. The collectives were broken up after the collapse of communism. This has led to the victimization of poor people. Land in the Kalniskes area is bought up by strong farmers and by wealthy people from Vilnius who build summer cottages.

Former President Landsbergis once visited the area. Michail scoffed that Landsbergis was surrounded by eight bodyguards and spent most of his time with the wealthy families.

Michail supplied the following genealogical details, which were new to us. Jonas Bielawski (1886-1946), his father and my grandfather's younger brother, married late because he had to marry off his stepsisters. This would indicate that the first Michail Bielawski, my great-grandfather, died approximately 1915. Michail knew his grandfather married a second time—to the awfully-named Rozalia Bagdruzil—but he had no knowledge of this lady. There are Bagdruzils in the vicinity of Kalniskes, but the families are not close.

Jonas and other local people were rounded up in World War Two and put in a building that was to be torched by the Nazis. For some reason this was not done and they survived, perhaps because the Soviet advance was approaching too rapidly.

The leading family in the region in the early part of the twentieth century was "Vyginski (phonetic)". Many of the local people worked for them. This family fled when the Soviets took over in World War Two. Their house, an unusual one made of brick, was bombed in the war.

The original intention was for Jonas to join his brothers in America, but he was sickly at the time and not allowed to board the steamship. (This would have been in the period 1910-14.) He had a farm of around thirteen hectares, but the government cut it back to ten hectares—this is about twenty-five American acres. After his death, the farm was divided between Michail and his sister Marija. At the time of Jonas's death in 1946, they were children.

The original Bielawski property in Kalniskes is now an empty field with linden trees on it. We did not get to visit.

Turgeli

Turgeli is the site of the Church of the Virgin Mary, the Roman Catholic parish for this region. The parish goes back to the sixteenth century. Written records commence from early in the nineteenth century.

The church, the fourth on the site, is an imposing building visible for miles. It is constructed of red, black, and gray bricks and mirror steeples on either side of the nave. Over the vestibule is a black design that resembles in outline the image of the Blessed Mother with hands and cloak extended. Higher over the door is a statue of Mary inserted in the wall. As is common in churches in Lithuania, the brick facade extends high over the roof.

Behind the back wall of the church is a statue of Jesus carrying the Cross. The statue, which is painted in vivid lifelike colors, stands on a pedestal some four feet or so off the ground. The statue comes as a pleasant surprise to anyone who walks around the building.

The somewhat ponderous appearance of the church may result from the steeples, which taper off very little as they ascend, and from the fact that the building stands at the confluence of three roads. As they disappear into the countryside, the roads become very narrow, in places hardly more than a lane in width; as they converge on the church the roads spill into a remarkably wide square. I imagine this space serves as a parking lot for the cars—and for the horses-and-buggies. Probably, the space also serves as a market.

The church in Turgeli exhibits a characteristic I observed in the churches in Vilnius. The exterior appears massive, but the interior is small and crowded. There is a double row of narrow wood pews in the center nave. For the life of me, I couldn't see how a grown man could kneel in one—maybe people are smaller here and have short legs. Five square columns stand on either side of the pews. Each column has a picture of a saint on it; they may be getting ahead of themselves, since a picture of John Paul II is on the first column. There are no pews on the exterior naves—this is also a characteristic of the churches in Vilnius. Several confessional boxes stand alongside the walls. These boxes are different than what we have in American churches. They are mere shells, lacking doors and curtains. The faces of both priest and penitent are exposed to public view. I don't know if a person can read sins by facial gestures—a grimace here and a frown there may disclose particular transgressions of commission and omission—but it may not be necessary to keep one's spectacles up-to-date. Since the confessionals lack roofs as well as walls, all you have to do is suck your gut in, squeeze in the pew, and wait for sound waves to carry notice how much better you are than your neighbor.

The interior of the building is painted white. The ceilings are tall and vaulted. A modern altar is turned toward the people, as in American churches, and there is a large crucifix over the old altar, which is set back from the communion rail.

While we visited a ceremony was in progress, possibly rehearsal for First Holy Communion. The little girls were in white dresses and the boys were smartly dressed in sweaters and pressed pants. An older man quizzed the children on the catechism. It's likely this man was a priest, but I can't say for sure, since he wasn't wearing vestments. He yelled questions at the children, picking them out individually, and they responded in quiet tones. I had to squint to hear what they were saying, but then I relaxed my eyebrows. I remembered they weren't speaking English.

Girdziunai

We traveled to Girdziunai, the ancestral home of the Storta and Juchniewicz families, on June 9. Once again, Irena was our translator and Kestas was our driver.

The trip took slightly more than an hour. Girdziunai is in extreme southeastern Lithuania in the little geographical comma or tail that hangs in what used to be Russia and is now the made-up nation of Belarus. The countryside between Vilnius and Salcininki, the nearest city of any size, is a great plain of flat pastureland. There's not an appreciable hill in sight and the timberline looks to be in another county—country, I should say, since the borders of three countries are close. The road meanders like a ribbon along this plain and for all the difference we might be driving on the Delmarva Peninsula. The few cultivated fields we passed were dirt plots reserved for tubers.

The scenery changes as we neared the Byelorussian border south of Salcininki, altering from grassland to heavy forest. Such deep woods—fir trees, mostly, and fir shrubbery—are what we would expect near Russia.

The road to the *kaimas* of Girdziunai opens at the literal border of Lithuania and Belarus. Two young soldiers in green uniforms sit in a shack outside a gate with a security arm. They seem friendly and make a cursory check of the van. Not exactly Checkpoint Charley, but exciting nevertheless. The road is dirt and in very bad condition since the fall of communism—it was probably in bad condition before the fall of communism. It runs for about a half mile, curving up and down through the deep woods. The soil is bright yellow. One side of the road is Lithuania, the other Belarus. If my arms were long enough, the van narrow enough, I could put my hands outside the window and say I was in two countries at the same time.

Girdziunai is a village of about twenty or thirty houses arranged close together on both sides of the road, which continues through the village and into the woods. Not all the houses are occupied; a fair number are empty. The houses resemble one another in structure and complexion, having a faded yellow appearance. Everything looks to be made of wood of the same age and quality. An unpainted serrated fence runs on either side of the road. It breaks only for walks and for driveways. The village is heavily forested, with considerable shade over the road.

There's an impressive quaintness about Girdziunai. I imagine I've stepped backwards into the nineteenth century. I think of the *clachan* of Ireland—I may as well be standing in nineteenth-century Derrynacong in County Mayo as in twentieth-century Girdziunai. And I think of Mark Twain's marvelous descriptions of similar towns in nineteenth-century America. I suppose such places, frozen in time, are much the same the world over.

Danislav Storta, Babci's first cousin, is a stocky man about six feet tall. He has thick jowly features, with deeply set eyes and ruddy cheeks. His hair is white and quite profuse. He is sixty-nine years of age. Unfortunately, his health is not good. His hands are quite large, swollen perhaps, and he is missing the tip of one of his fingers. He has a paunch and carries all his weight in his midsection. He has heart arrhythmia and a condition that sounds like a stomach hernia. He breathes loudly, as if he was always in a hurry, and has a remarkably deep voice. He uses glasses to read.

Danislav's wife is a short woman in her sixties. Like him, she has a ruddled complexion. She wears a simple dark dress and a kerchief.

Josef, their son, is about the same height as his father and has a solid build. His hair is brown and cut thin. He resembles his mother more than Danislav. He says little during our visit. Josef's wife is a short woman. She is heavyset and, contrary to her husband, has an outgoing personality. She works as a nurse. They have two children. Their oldest, a girl about twelve, is tall with short hair. Their youngest is a blond girl around eight or nine. She is being treated for measles and has a blue ointment dotting her face.

The Stortas have two daughters. Teresa is a stocky woman around thirty. (A lot of people in Girdziunai are on the stocky side. Life must have been good in these parts under communism—maybe it was the kielbasa.) Her hair is blond. She has one daughter.

Janina, the second daughter, is a medical doctor in Salcininki Hospital. She also has blond hair and is taller than her sister. She has an uncanny facial similarity to my sister Felicia, although she is fuller of feature. She is married to a pleasant red-faced man with black hair and a mustache. My impression is that her husband is a professional man, but he didn't say anything, so it's difficult to tell.

Janina is curious about the medical profession in America, asking about salaries and quality of treatment. For some reason, she's especially curious about how we treat indigent people. She admits she doesn't have many more instruments than a stethoscope and blood-pressure gauge, but she's proud of the fact that her diagnoses are usually confirmed by the better equipped hospitals in Vilnius.

Janina has two children, a blond daughter around five years and a son around seven. This boy is much darker and sharper of feature than his cousins. Curious but shy, he lingers near his grandfather. He may be the favorite, since he's allowed to stay on his grandfather's lap as the adults converse.

The Storta homestead is arranged as follows. The house is to the left of the gate. A tractor is parked at the entrance of the gate. The entrance to the house is at the rear. Immediately behind the house is an indoors garden constructed of wood, wire, and a plastic cover that looks like it can be rolled back and forth to control the light. Behind the garden is an enormous pile of wood chopped into one or two foot segments. Across from the wood is a barn-like structure of singular construction. The exterior wall of this structure is reinforced by the same stock of wood as in the pile. To the rear of the woodpile is a cul-de-sac leading to a traditional barn. A number of henhouses extend in the woods behind this barn. There's an outhouse in the vicinity—there is no indoor plumbing.

Danislav's father was named Matweg, which is Russian for Matthew. No one in our family in America knew he existed until we discovered him in the ships' logs microfilmed in the National Archives on Houston St. in Manhattan. Matweg entered the United States in 1909 and returned to Lithuania in 1914. Now, there are small mistakes in life and there are large mistakes, and Matweg made a large mistake returning, considering the disparate histories of Jersey City and Girdziunai in the twentieth century. Regardless of this decision, Matweg played an important role in our family, since he introduced my grandparents.

Danislav disclosed some details of his father's life. When Matweg returned to Girdziunai he served in the Russian army and was captured by the Germans in World War One. He spent considerable time as a prisoner-of-war. He married a woman named Paulina, who survived him by many years. They married in 1922. Matweg died in 1934, aged fifty two, so he would have been born around 1882.

Matweg was a farmer, having ten hectares of land. He was an excellent fisherman and carpenter. Danislav proudly announced that he had built the house we sat in.

Danislav had heard that his father worked on a barge when he lived in Jersey City. That is plausible, since Matweg lived on Provost St., which was on the Hudson River waterfront. Most of Provost St. has since disappeared into the Newport Mall complex.

Danislav remembered that a village elder told him that the original Storta settler in Girdziunai arrived after the Russian-Swedish war. There were two such wars in the eighteenth century, the larger one around 1710, the smaller one around 1790. (The Storta family is documented in Girdziunai in church records since 1801.) Danislav had also been told that the original Storta was not Slavic but French or American. The latter possibility seems unlikely, but the former is quite possible, since Russia employed mercenaries of all nationalities, including French, to supplement their army. Intriguingly, there is a French word *Storto* meaning "one-eyed" and pronounced *Stort-ta*. Stanley Storta, my mother's uncle, had a condition in which one eye turned white. However, no other relatives have exhibited such a condition to my knowledge.

Danislav did not know who the local chieftains were in the nineteenth century. He related that the major industrialist in the years before World War Two was a man named Wagner, who owned a distillery in Salcininki. The distillery was built of brick and withstood bombing during the war. During

Gorbachev's time, the building was converted into a dairy as part of an anti-alcoholism campaign.

The notion of an anti-alcohol campaign amused our hosts. Mrs. Storta left the room and returned with a decanter of what American backwoodsmen call *moonshine*. Distilled from grain, this homemade liquor was clear as vodka but tasted like whiskey. I sipped it carefully, since I had already tried wine, brandy, and champagne, and thought it wasn't a good idea to continue to mix "the grape with the grain".

Like the Bielawski family, the Stortas served a huge meal. This meal included chicken, ham, herring, homemade bread, tomatoes and cucumbers, potatoes and dumplings, galumpis, and pickles. (Danislav didn't seem especially proud of the pickles.) I don't eat meat, so I had to stay with the vegetables, and there were plenty of those. There were also the aforementioned liquors. I did not vote for President Gorbachev.

We didn't see much of the Storta house. The door was on the right side of the building. We passed quickly through the kitchen and through a small second room and proceeded directly into the main parlor. This room was unusually large. There was a fireplace to the left. A large table stood at the center. An overhead light fixture hung over the table. A long couch, covered with a black cloth, was behind the table. A large glass cabinet, constructed of dark wood, stood against the left wall. There were two windows in the wall behind the couch and two additional windows in the wall opposite the cabinets. Danislav's wedding picture hung on the wall, as did a picture of the Blessed Mother.

I asked Danislav about conditions in Girdziunai and in Lithuania. He said that this period matched the uncertainties and the troubles—but without the persecutions and the killings—that followed World War Two. He admitted that people in the region had settled into a comfortable, but poor, life style under communism centered around the collective farm. He thought they would be able to adjust again, although it would take time. From what I saw, they had adjusted quite well. His daughter was a doctor, his daughter-in-law was a nurse, and they had considerably more amenities than I expected.

Danislav said that merchants and farmers sometimes underwent strong-arm tactics by young people, who had no work, except as criminals. The police ignored such extortion because they were paid off. His comments seemed to be based on personal experience and to touch his family, since there was considerable chatting when he spoke of the criminal element.

He claimed that the people in Girdziunai were not especially political. In fact, he claimed that their unique characteristic was their lack of interest in politics. He added that many people in Girdziunai suffer with a "disorder in the feet", which is rather unspecific. It was not clear whether he referred to circulation problems or to some kind of infectious disease. He attributed this disorder to radiation from the Chernobyl catastrophe. We traveled four thousand miles to hear this story and Chernobyl is five hundred miles from Girdziunai. These facts are proof that the world has become a very small place.

Vilnius

The experience of traveling from Helsinki to Vilnius was a novel one. We rode in a thirty-four seat propeller plane. It was the first propeller plane I ever flew in. I have no complaints, however. The ride was surprisingly smooth. We didn't drop out of the sky as I thought we would and the Hail Marys I said on take off and landing must count for something in the airport in the afterworld.

Even though we were in the air for an hour, alcohol in all sizes and proofs was available gratis—all right, not gratis, as the drinks came with the cost of the ticket, but you didn't have to unhitch your seat belt and reach into your pocket like you do on American flights. I hear tell the three people in first class were flying high, but this is only a rumor, as my seat was last in the aisle and next to the toilet. I didn't avail myself of any beverages, since I had to stay dry in the event the plane ditched in the Baltic Sea and I needed to swim to Klaipeda.

The plane landed safely and I and thirty-three other people, some of whom were pretty sloshed, lived to tell the story.

This comparison is not altogether correct, but Vilnius reminded me of Dallas. The reason for the comparison isn't hard to come by. Both cities contain the most amazing contrasts in architecture. On one side of the street is a drab stone building of five stories. Across the street is a modern glass box transported from Elm and Houston Sts. Down the block is an eighteenth-century church. Next to it is a black brick high rise with balconies. On the other side of the street is a barn-like structure made of wood.

The Old Town in Vilnius contains buildings—mostly churches—of great age and beauty. Vilnius also has its share of Texas eyesores. There's a particularly ugly building visible from the hotel window. It's the twenty-two story Hotel Lietuva, which was the international meeting place in the Soviet era. Besides its monstrous height, which is out of all proportion to its neighbors, it has an immense sign on the roof. The sign glows "H-O-T-E-L" in alternating red, green, and white colors. True, the colors are Lithuania's, but so tall and dull a building, capped by so tacky a billboard, could stand without apologies in downtown Dallas.

We stayed at the Hotel Naujasis Vilnius, which is on a steep hill close to the north bank of the Neris River. It's a drab building, although it has a first-class restaurant with an enormous menu. The rooms are tiny and offer no view, other than the Hotel Lietuva, which is no view at all. Oh, for the days of the Dallas Reunion, when I could look out on Dealey Plaza and ponder just who killed President Kennedy.

The clash of architecture is obvious once you step outside and walk to the bridge that leads to the Old Town. There is an American-style supermarket to the right of the hotel, with bakery and liquor store attached. To the left is a Planetarium, of all things. The Planetarium has a silver dome of rather small size—Lithuania is a small country with a small night sky. Across from the supermarket is an immense three-story department store. Rather, it's a vast shell of a building in which merchants rent space to sell their wares flea-market style. A quick tour revealed that the wares are the same in every booth, mostly cheap jewelry and expensive cosmetics.

Across from the Planetarium is the Church of St. Raphael. The church is rather run down on the exterior. A few beggars sit near the entrance. But the church has a pleasant courtyard, which is enclosed and not visible from the street, and it has two steeples that are visible for a considerable distance. The church is very bright and pretty on the inside. It's as if the clergy spent all the collection money repairing the interior to the detriment of the exterior. Not a bad idea in religious circles.

In many ways St. Raphael resembles the Church of the Virgin Mary in Turgeli. It's much smaller on the inside than it looks on the outside. It has considerable ornamentation and a small and heavily decorated altar. The pulpit is raised and the pews are made of wood and located in the center nave. There are two side altars alongside the walls. The exterior walls contain the Stations of the Cross. They also contain those unique open confessionals.

As aside about Lithuanian beggars. We had expected to be besieged by members of the beggar class. In fact, the situation is no worse in the Old Town of Vilnius than it is in the midtown of Manhattan. Most of the beggars we saw in Vilnius were congregated near the entrances of churches. Most were elderly women dressed in black, although there was an occasional middle-aged man. Regardless, they were polite and quiet. They tended to sit on the ground with hands, caps, or cups, outstretched. They mumble appeals and then gratitude, more loudly and with frequent bows and obviously faked emotion, as they catch visitors in and out from worship. The exceptions to this well-mannered system are school-age children. These urchins, who are clean and dressed neatly, race up as soon as they spot you and appeal, "*Litas, litas*", *litas* being the national currency, presently valued at four-to-a-dollar. A few children offer postcards, which never change hands. Occasionally, one will mumble words to the effect, "brother, brother", the gist being brother doesn't have long for this world. The response of these children to the presence of tourists is so spontaneous, it reminded me of classical conditioning, although of a higher-order variety. Their activity doesn't bode well for the future of Lithuanian capitalism.

We paid a visit to the Church of St. Peter and Paul on Sunday morning. This church, a national landmark, is considered one of the most beautiful in the country. It is situated slightly north of town on the south bank of the Neris River. Like most of the churches in Lithuania, it's quite plain on the outside, although there is a faded painting of the Blessed Mother located on one of the outside walls. The building, which is large and nearly windowless, resembles a private residence or museum as much as it does a church. But the interior of this church is breathtakingly beautiful.

The walls and ceiling of the church are brilliantly white and covered with two-thousand figures of religious and natural scenes. The figures appear to be marble, but they are, in fact, painted gypsum. Whatever their composition, they are an amazing sight. I have never seen a Catholic church so gaudy with ornamentation. But "gaudy" is not the right word, since the interior is perfectly stylized and harmonious. It's no insult, but an eye-biting feast.

To the left of the altar, about halfway down and raised over the pews, is a carved pulpit. There is an awning over the pulpit. An angel sits on the awning. There is also a lectern complete with sculptured book. A floral design covers the front of the pulpit.

Close to the altar and elevated slightly higher than eye level is a most remarkable chandelier. It is a delicate model, like lace almost, of a sailing vessel. I have no idea what its significance is, or what its place could be in a church, but we could not inspect it close up, since high mass was in progress. (We entered to a rousing chorus of *Kyrie eleison*.) The church was crowded to overflowing. People stood in the very narrow pews, along the side aisles, and in the portal. A row of benches outside the church was also filled to capacity. The mass was broadcast on loudspeakers to the crowd outside—the quality wasn't very good. The people on the outside stood, sat, and knelt in accordance with the ceremony.

Inside the church, about midway up on the right wall, is a small chapel dedicated to St. Ursula. I visited despite the mass, since one of my great-grandmother's names was Ursula. Unfortunately, the chapel is not remarkable. It contains a plain altar with a large statue of Mary in place of a tabernacle.

The church is supposed to stand on the site of a pagan temple. It was established by a local chieftain at the end of the seventeenth century. It has stood witness to many tragedies in Lithuanian history. Many tragedies are part of ancient history, and no one really cares about them, since the twentieth century has seen more tragedies on vaster scales than any in olden times. But one tragedy is very much a part of modern Lithuanian history and very much a part of the consciousness of the citizenry. More than seven hundred victims of KGB justice were found buried near the church in what is now a park on the Neris River. (In those years the park had been a private estate.) These unfortunates, buried without prayers in unhallowed ground, were killed in KGB headquarters located on Gedimino St. in the center of town.

It is possible to visit the former KGB headquarters. During World War Two the building served as Gestapo headquarters. The building is now called the Museum of Genocide. Thousands of people were tortured and killed inside. As can be imagined, it is a sad and sinister place.

The building is a huge, castle-like structure located near the modern Parliament. It stands across the street from a large treeless park. A colossal statue of Lenin, the sociopath who founded the system that gave the world as institution like the KGB, once stood in the park. The statue went the way of the Tsars when Lithuania gained its independence.

Entrance to the cells where a century of atrocities were committed is on the side street. Stairs descend one flight to the basement. A door opens to an immense corridor that progresses nearly the block-long length of the building. The walls of the corridor are dirty and painted an insipid green and beige. The corridor is narrow, probably not more than five feet across. Bare hanging bulbs provide a hint of illumination.

Rows of doors, more than twenty, maybe as many as fifty, opened on both sides of the corridor. It is a corridor of death, and the doors open to the rooms of death.

To the immediate left of the stairs are two doors that opened to holding pens. But "pens" can't be the right word, since they are not much larger than walk-in closets. Here, prisoners were kept until they were *processed*.

The first few doors thereafter opened to KGB officialdom, but they may as well have opened to hell. One room was the receiving area, another was reserved for the commandant, a third for the guards, a fourth for the photographing and fingerprinting of prisoners.

As we continued along the corridor, ever deeper into the building, the doors opened to prison cells. The cells are about fifteen feet deep and ten feet wide. Each door contains an aperture about six inches in width through which meals could be passed. Inside, there are bare benches along the walls and what appear to be bedpans built into the floor. The benches served for beds. I do not know if the furniture is original.

Our guide was an elderly gentleman who indicated he had been exiled to Siberia after spending time in these cells. He pointed to graffiti on the wall in one cell. I couldn't make out the writing, except for one name written in large letters. The letters read "Helen B – 40". For what it's worth after these years, may God bless Helen B.

I don't remember windows in any of the cells, and I didn't feel comfortable photographing interiors as our guide stood near. It seemed profane to do so. A few cells had tiny desks or what looked like nightstands between benches. One cell had a large portrait of a bishop who had been killed here and buried in the park near Sts. Peter and Paul.

I've always had a personal belief, an intuition or a suspicion, that hell is not hot, as we've been told, but cold. (This belief may have arisen from waiting for too many buses in cold weather.) This place was a kind of hell, and it feels cold, despite the fact that we're one floor below street level on an eighty-degree day. It's cold and clammy, and there's an unpleasant odor, slightly metallic and damp, such as hangs in rooms that are sealed shut for too long.

As we progressed the corridor turned sharply to the left and then to the right. The cells were no less numerous in this portion and their implications became more obviously brutal.

In the bend of the corridor there is a padded cell, presumably for prisoners who went insane. Near it, there is a chamber our guide designated as "the punishment cell". This chamber is a very small room, about half the size of the cells. There is a bench attached to the back wall. The bedpan-like contraption is on the floor to the left of the door.

There are two punishment chambers in this section that provide architectural evidence that my conjecture about hell may be correct. These chambers were used for ice water tortures in winter. They are sunken rooms whose floors are two feet lower than the corridor. They are devoid of furniture except for a circular faucet in the middle of the room.

We saw one execution chamber. We climbed back to ground level, exiting the building into an interior courtyard. (We were separated from the street by a large wooden door more than a story tall.) There was an entrance into the adjoining portion of building about thirty feet from where we emerged. This entrance was sealed with two chained boards that served as gates. The boards did not close completely and could be separated a few inches by scraping them along the ground. The entrance opened into a square chamber maybe twenty feet wide ending in a flight of stairs that led back down to the subterranean level. The corridor at the foot of the stairs was painted bright yellow and the area was in disarray with a lot of wood lying around.

Our guide produced a scrap of paper on which were numbered years starting with 1944 and ending with 1948. Next to each year were the number of executions carried out in this courtyard. The total was in the hundreds.

I wondered why the executions occurred above ground when all the torture occurred below ground, and the answer was obvious. The prisoners could walk to their executions. Their bodies didn't have to be dragged up a flight of stairs in defiance of gravity but could be thrown on lorries and brought to the burial ground.

The Academy of Music was across the street from the KGB headquarters. The musicians referred to the frequent shootings as "the percussion section" of the orchestra.

Before I leave this awful topic I should mention three additional chambers. One, located within the building near the stairs leading to the courtyard, is the "exercise room". This room is a large chamber with a central block of metal. Prisoners were allowed a period of exercise within this enclosed space. Said exercise amounted to circumambulations around the block.

Another chamber, located closer to the cells, is the shower. This is a small room in which prisoners were allowed to wash every ten days. The walls look like faded porcelain. The tiles resembled a subway billboard bereft of messages.

Finally, there is a room near the zigzag of the corridor that served as a pillbox. Three small windows open at the level of the sidewalk. Thick horizontal bars cover the windows, which are wire rather than glass. Below the windows are benches on which KGB officers could position themselves in the event the building was attacked.

KGB headquarters is a terribly gloomy place to visit. It is a monument to the cruelties people inflict on one another in the name of a political system. The only satisfaction walking through such a miserable place is to realize that the rotten systems that sent so many people to their deaths have themselves joined the funeral heap of history.

The heart of Vilnius is situated along two thoroughfares, one quite modern and crowded with traffic, the other medieval and mostly closed to vehicles. The former, Gedimino *Gatve* ("street" in Lithuanian), runs west to east. The latter, Pilies *Gatve*, runs north to south.

Parliament is at the western end of Gedimino St. The building is a modern box, golden in color, and with considerable glass. The Lithuanian flag was aloft the day we visited, which indicated that President Brazauskas was in. We did not get invited in for sweets or meats.

Directly next to Parliament and separated from it by a plaza is the National Library, an immense building of dark stone and a huge staircase some two or three stories tall. The building looked positively forbidding to young scholars—it gave the glum message *there is no joy in scholarship*—and the stairs looked fatal to scholars of advanced years. If ever a building was in need of an escalator, it was this place.

Midway on Gedimino St. is a godsend to Americans, a little piece of home to homesick travelers, and an oasis where the hungry can buy a burger and fries and get a cup of *kavos* (coffee). Of course, I refer to McDonald's. It's the only one in Vilnius, maybe the only one in Lithuania. And it's mine every time I pass. There's nothing like the smell of overcooked coffee roasting in a Styrofoam cup. It smells like—like America.

Some people take the highbrow attitude that the presence of the yellow arch is a disgrace in so historic a thoroughfare and Irena told us that most Lithuanians couldn't afford to eat there, but I don't think either observation is entirely true. There were several expensive stores and restaurants on Gedimino St., so the area is not off limits to free enterprise. KBG headquarters lurks a few blocks away, and if a blot on the reputation of humanity can stand in the center of town, so can McDonald's. (It's unimaginable conceiving a place like McDonald's serving fries, burgers, and coffee in the same period the KBG served beatings, ice water, and bullets—who can deny times haven't changed for the better?) The place was crowded every time we stopped in a for a caffeine recharge. I saw decrepit old-timers hobbling onto the line and a battalion of mothers and children, their carriages serving for wagons. There were, in addition, numerous couples starting their dates with Big Macs and groups of well-dressed young Balts lounging at outdoor tables with their shakes, cigarettes, and fries, quite as if they were enjoying the most exclusive of cafes.

McDonald's fulfilled my need to walk around town carrying a Styrofoam cup of *kavos*—this is a need honed on the streets of the great Manhattan. The last thing I missed from home was the sight and sound of baseball or anything related to baseball. I observed neither ball nor bat, and there wasn't a ballpark in sight. Kids weren't having a catch. Americans know they're in a foreign land when there are no ballparks. If it wasn't for the yellow arch, a fellow could get mighty lonely.

Gedimino *Gatve* concludes to the east at Cathedral Square. There is a small restaurant at the intersection in the front of the Cathedral, the Literary Café (*Literatu Svetaine*), that is of some interest. It was from this café that the poet Czeslaw Milosz witnessed Soviet troops entering Vilnius in June, 1940. We sat at an outdoor table and enjoyed beer, salads, and coffee. I'm happy to report that no troops invaded while we dined.

The Cathedral of St. Stanislaw is the most imposing building in Vilnius. It is the center of religious life and, in the years before Lithuania obtained its independence, of political life, as well. The history of the site goes back to pagan times, when a temple to the god of thunder stood here. The history of Christian churches dates to the late twelfth century. During the years of Lithuania's expansion into an empire, the site was part of a castle complex centered around the steep hill behind the Cathedral. The current building dates from 1784.

The Cathedral is an immense rectangle of a building extending for what seems the length of a football field. The building is stark white, with no hint of any other color; it was cleaned in 1993 for the Pope's visit. There are six huge columns at the entrance. There are several statues embedded in the walls along the front and sides. They represent a mixture of political and spiritual characters, although you can't tell them apart. There are three statues poised on the ledge of the roof.

The interior of the Cathedral is excessively grand. The high altar is a city block away; maybe they issue opera glasses with the hymnals. Square columns section off the interior into three naves. As in other churches, only the center nave contains pews. As befits a Cathedral, the pews are wider than in diocesan churches. A long-legged fellow could kneel with room for an umbrella.

There are several chapels along the exterior walls of the Cathedral. Each is like a small church, with altar, pews, artwork, and candle racks. The ceilings in the chapels are nearly as tall as the ceiling in the center nave, which gives them an odd tubular appearance.

All the chapels are impressive, but the outstanding one is that of St. Casimir, the patron saint of Lithuania. (Casimir is buried in the Cathedral.) This chapel is considered the premier example of Baroque art in the country. The walls are dark granite and marble, creating a black and silver appearance. The walls and ceilings contain frescoes detailing the saint's life. All are rich in color. There are large statues of Casimir near the corners of the chapel. The effect is remarkable, but the statues themselves are deceptive, since they are wood with silver plating and not silver throughout. To see so much art in so confined a space is nearly overwhelming. It's like seeing a cameo or some kind of spiritual palace; rather, it's like being inside a cameo, the effect is so intense.

There were several elderly ladies in the chapel, bumping their gums and thumbing the rosary. They wore housedresses and babushkas, and they weren't beautiful at all, being old and ugly. But in a strange way they belonged amid the stark beauty of the room. It was a case of beauty and the babushkas.

Outside the Cathedral, across the street from the Literary Salon, stands a famous bell tower. The base of the tower dates back to the castle complex of the thirteenth century. The rest of the tower was added incrementally over the centuries, with the last restoration in the nineteenth century. The clock still functions, although it was set over two hundred years ago.

The bell tower resembles a lighthouse in height and structure. In olden times it was used as a lookout for invaders—Lord knows, there were enough of them— and as a fire watch. The only ships the tower now has to guide go on four wheels and cross tar lanes, and that's a chore, since Gedimino *Gatve* curves sharply at this point and vehicles take the curve at high rates of speeds. It's a miracle the belfry, which has withstood centuries of martial and natural abuse, hasn't been flattened by a motor vehicle.

Directly behind the Cathedral is Castle Hill, which rises dramatically over street level. Ruins of a fourteenth century Gothic structure stand on the hill. Excavations are in progress. A sixty-foot octagonal tower has been restored and can be entered and climbed for a small fee. This tower, built of orange brick, offers an outstanding view of Vilnius. It is possible to see for miles. I don't think I would have liked to be on the tower during an invasion—"Here come the Teutonic Knights!" "Here come the Tartars!" "Here come the Swedes!" "Here come the Russians!" "Here come the Germans!" "Here come the Russians again!"

My present duties at Barnes & Noble involve maintaining the used book stock of the former Sale Annex, once located at 18th St. & Fifth Ave. In a manner of speaking, I'm the curator of two hundred thousand used books; you might say I have my private used book depository. So, I could not resist visiting the English-language used bookstore—*rutos knygos*—located across the street from the Cathedral. But "store" isn't the correct word, since the space wasn't much larger than someone's living room. Quite possibly, it had been someone's living room.

The store consisted of a few panels of books arranged by subject and a table or two of mass market paperbacks. The selection wasn't first-rate—no Karl Popper or Kennedy assassination literature—but I am a person with access to two hundred thousand volumes. What the store lacked in merchandise it made up in customers. The store was crowded with browsers, although six people would have been a crowd in that place.

Two women sat at the entrance of the store. I took the younger one for the saleslady, the older one for a customer. Of all movable things on earth, an oversized Barnes & Noble shopping bag was at her feet. I felt more at home seeing that bag than if I ordered an extra-large container of *kavos* at McDonald's. I felt so much at home, I reached for my name tag and thought to ask if they wanted me to sign on the cash register.

I inquired about the shopping bag and tried to communicate that I was a Barnes & Noble employee, one of the last men standing in *rutos knygos*, but it was no use. *Jos nesupranta*—they did not understand. The younger lady spoke no English and the older one, who spoke with a British accent, hadn't the foggiest notion that Barnes & Noble existed. I could have mentioned that she had only to look at the bag at her feet, but I didn't want to sound like an ugly American.

It's a short walk from the bookstore to Pilies *Gatve*, which is the center of the Old Town. Pilies St. commences at Kalnu Park behind the Cathedral—this park lies at the base of Castle Hill—and concludes at the Dawn Gate about a mile distant. The street forks several times as it meanders to the south. Each time it forks, it changes names; for the sake of simplicity, I will refer to the entire stretch as Pilies St., which is all I ever knew it as.

The western end consists of a narrow, somewhat claustrophobic, cobblestone path flanked by old and rundown buildings, all two and three stories tall and continuous one with the other. Many of these buildings are under restoration. Their faces are mostly brick in various states of disrepair, and they have small metal placards in Lithuanian declaring what's in store for them. I could make out the single word "Architecture". Since I am in the *old* part of the Old Town, I suppose they are considered landmarks.

Many of these buildings are arranged in an architectural style I will call in my ignorance "backside first", since the entrances to them are gained not on Pilies St. but through common courtyards or alleys. Entrances into these courtyards are usually made through heavy wood doors. These doors rarely stand parallel with the ground but always seem to be careening in one direction or the other. This pattern—of presenting the backs of houses to the thoroughfares and of placing the entrances on the sides facing away—is common in the Old Town and I observed it in Girdziunai, which is as far from the Old Town as we can go without leaving Lithuania.

One of these courtyards may be said to be a trick courtyard, opening not to a cul-de-sac ringed by crooked doors but to a cluster of small and undistinguished buildings that comprise Vilnius University. The university was founded in 1579, which makes it one of the oldest in the world, but the campus is not impressive. It consists of a confusing complex of plain-looking low buildings, many of which are whitewashed or left with the masonry showing. Some of the buildings, dormitories most likely, had books on the windowsills. One building was a glass-and-steel modern structure. It had a staircase that ran along the entire front entrance. For some reason, I took this building for a library.

A considerable number of young people were on the streets. Some were carrying books or folders. All were nicely dressed. There were also a number of middle-aged gents strolling about. Most had thick glasses; a few had gray beards. Obviously, they were professors; probably, they were former socialists converted to the new religion of capitalism.

Pilies St. widens as it proceeds to the south and the buildings become more modern, with a richness of color not often seen on American main streets. The buildings are painted bright yellow and red and pink. One of the most striking is a tall church situated about midway on our walk. The brick façade is broken, but the church is painted a startling pink. Unfortunately, the church was closed, so we could not observe the interior.

Near the campus of Vilnius University is an open-air flea market consisting of a line of booths, all of which sell the same items at much the same prices. Amber products are featured, either raw or set in jewelry or in religious bric-a-brac. The proprietors of the booths make their appeals in broken English. "Ver-ree nice" is the preferred phrase. "Ver-ree inn-teresting piece" is also common. They point out that many samples of amber come with microscopic foliage or insects entombed inside. They offer magnifying lenses to show the insects.

I don't know for a fact whether amber regularly contains microscopic insects – I like to think the piece I bought does—but amber is a rich color, sometimes pale yellow, sometimes brandy-orange, ver-ree pleasing to the eyes. I couldn't resist their appeals. Besides, I didn't travel four thousand miles *not* to buy amber products with or without insects.

The proprietors are very friendly and motivated to turn a sale—they even engage in suggestive selling. However, there was one booth, located in a courtyard across the street from the flea market, whose proprietors had not gotten the knack of capitalism. Whether this was by choice, I don't know.

An elderly couple stood by their wares in the courtyard. The woman was a stereotypical babushka. She stood four feet nine in longitude and four foot seven in latitude and she wore, despite the heat, a sweater, ankle-long skirt of some kind of flannel material, and the required kerchief. The man bore a strong resemblance to First Secretary Brezhnev. He was tall and stout, with thick black hair, obviously dyed, and stringy black eyebrows, also dyed. His face was long and puffy, the jaw taking up half the head. He wore a threadbare green suit buttoned to the collar. He stood at attention at the side of the table. Neither he nor the old lady acknowledged that customers had wandered in.

They sold a number of coins and military objects. On the table were several large rocks, one literally the size of a suitcase; perhaps they were shells or the remnants of shells. The featured items were two large portraits of Marshal Stalin placed on rickety chairs in front of the table. In one portrait the Great Father stares directly at the viewer. In the other the Great Father is in profile; he wears a military uniform and is surrounded by a halo.

My guess is that this couple was down on their luck and forced, like the late First Secretary's widow, to sell the military decorations and objects of communist art that had inspired them in better years. Their reserve and hidden location may have reflected their shame in having to kowtow to the new god on the bloc.

I was tempted to buy one of the portraits, but I declined. I was rather embarrassed when I entered the courtyard and I doubted I could get the portrait through customs so soon after the fall of the state religion. I could pretend I was a collector of historical art or of historical curiosities, but I thought better of making the attempt. The Great Father was where he belonged—in a hole-in-the wall attended by decrepit devotees on death's doorstep.

A short walk from the flea market leads to the historic Town Square, which is a wide triangular stretch bordered on the sides by stores and by those brightly-colored buildings and at the base by a large, museum-like building that serves as the Art Museum of Lithuania. This structure stands on what had been the site of the medieval town hall. It was built in the late eighteenth century on a rather monumental scale that included a portico with six columns.

In olden days the square served as the site of a large market that attracted farmers and tradesmen from as far away as Poland and Russia. The square also served as the center of communal life in the Old Town and as the place of public punishments and public executions—it was a busy place in the latter capacity in the nineteenth century. In present days the square attracts a different class of people—tourists, mostly, and Lithuanian yuppies who hang out at the very upscale bars and restaurants in the area. There are no executions, if one excludes the drinking crowd getting strung out.

Vilnius is a city of churches, a fact never more obvious than along Pilies St. There are at least seven churches in this circumscribed area; several, however, are under repair and not accessible to the public.

St. John's is a large, clay-colored church standing on its site since the fourteenth century. The present structure, dating from the late eighteenth century, is in the Baroque style. During the Soviet occupation St. John's was ravaged and dedicated as the Museum of Science. It was re-consecrated in 1991 and serves as the student church for the university. Next to the church is a large bell tower also dating to the eighteenth century. This bell tower, which is similarly clay-colored, is some five or six stories tall and serves as a landmark defining the center of the Old Town.

There are two Russian Orthodox churches west of the Town Square. (In Soviet days all religions were outlawed; in Tsarist times all religions except the Orthodox Church were squashed. This repression can be seen in church records of the mid-nineteenth century, which had to be recorded in Russian rather than in the native Lithuanian or regional Polish.) Both churches were large and under repair. The interior of one was blocked by scaffolding, so we couldn't get inside. This was unfortunate, because the walls were dark green in color. I don't know if the walls were originally this color, or if the color was added during renovation, but it's wonderful to see a green church in any denomination.

The other church—the Church of the Holy Spirit—is situated off the street in a small enclosed park. When we arrived, there were two priests standing at the door to the church. As we approached a few construction workers were exiting from the church. These workers stopped, bowed, and kissed the priests' hands. We didn't see any money exchange hands. Nor did we exchange money—or kisses—as we entered. But then, we're Americans, we don't kiss anyone's hand.

The interior of the church is beautiful, despite the scaffolding that occupies the center nave. The side naves, which have been restored, are filled to heavenly capacity with candle racks, frescoes, and portraits. I don't believe there was an empty space on the walls. Included among the certified saints are portraits of former monks and bishops, all of whom appeared to have reached enormous longevities, as measured by the length of their white beards.

The Roman Catholic Church of the Basilian Monastery is another holy place under repair. This church is reached by entering an alley that curves round to a cul-de-sac. Like the church, the nearby buildings are in disrepair. One building, which has the usual crooked door in front, carries a plaque dedicated to the poet Adam Mickiewicz, who resided here for a time in the nineteenth century. Shielded from the congestion on Pilies *Gatve*, the alley possesses a haunted and hushed quality. More than anyplace we visited in Vilnius, the alley looks old and feels old. We could almost watch the medieval epoch crumble before our eyes.

The church is in bad shape. The walls are scraped and broken, the statuary replaced by ivy. The steps are similarly fractured, with concrete plates lying lopsidedly about. It's not possible to enter the church, since the interior consists entirely of scaffolding. The interior was dark, so it was not possible to see beyond the inadequate daylight carried through the doorway.

Several icons hang on the scaffolding. One is of the Blessed Mother. Another is a large bright portrait of John Paul II. The pope wears his white cassock and skull cap and has a smile on his rosy-colored face. The smile of a Polish pope in a ruined Lithuanian church undergoing repair after decades of communist rule is not with obvious symbolism. Christ teaches forgiveness, but John Paul's portrait has an undisguised "he-who-laughs-last" quality.

Pilies St. concludes in yet another church—shrine, really. This is the Chapel of Our Lady of Vilnius. The shrine, which is a place of pilgrimage, contains a painting of the Black Madonna believed to possess powers of healing. The painting is kept in a small room located atop the Dawn Gate. Situated in an archway directly over Pilies St., the chapel affords an outstanding view of the Old Town.

The entrance is an unmarked, rather nondescript, crooked door located half a block away. To enter you have to clear a file of beggars who wait at the door. The beggars are rather passive, standing with hands outstretched and bobbing in an avian manner. One fellow, who may be king of the flock, had the habit of opening the door for the convenience of pilgrims. This is an effective gimmick in soliciting alms and one I have seen practiced in Manhattan, notably at the post office near the National Archives. I have to assume the practice evolved independently in Lithuania.

Once inside, pilgrims must climb several rather steep flights to reach the chapel. The painting may possess miraculous powers, but there is a selection factor operating. If you can climb the stairs without passing out or passing away, you're probably not in need of healing.

The chapel itself is a small room. There is a raised altar on the wall opposite the window that overlooks the street. The painting of the Black Madonna hangs over the altar. Mary is dark-skinned, dressed in gold, and surrounded by an immense number of flowers, candles, and votive offerings resting on the altar. The icon looked more like bas-relief than like paint to me, but it may be the severe contrast of color that caused the distortion. The icon has been here since 1671.

While we visited a distinguished bald gentleman in suit and tie was deep in prayer on the kneeler in front of the altar. He looked rather healthy—maybe he was praying for a cure for baldness.

The Dawn Gate is all that remains of the sixteenth century walls of the Old Town. There is no gate per se—and not a moat or drawbridge in sight—but a rather dark passage at the base of a massive, windowless chunk of a building. The passage is occupied by merchants selling religious items, mostly candles and amber rosary beads of the five-and-dime variety. The passage leads to the exterior of the Old Town and to traffic, noise, and packs of pedestrians rushing on business. In short, it leads to the twentieth century.

A multilingual pun—whenever I heard the word *Aciu*, which is "thank you" in Lithuanian and pronounced like a sneeze, I was tempted to say, "God bless you."

My taste in food runs from the bland to the ordinary—I avoid fish, fowl, and flesh—but I found the food in Vilnius highly satisfactory. The portions are generous and the price is right. A full dinner, with beer included, costs about forty *litas*, which sounds like a lot of money, but is only ten American dollars.

The gamut of cuisine runs from local Baltic dishes to Japanese and Chinese take-out. There are even Irish pubs serving Irish cuisine, insofar as

Irish food qualifies as cuisine. I tended to stay with Italian dishes, which are always safe choices. There was plenty of pasta to be found, mostly because the Italian embassy is located near the Town Square. With all the churches in town, there must be a circuit of papal nuncios making the rounds.

The best cuisine we sampled was at the Hotel Naujasis Vilnius. The menu was enormous and all the dishes were freshly prepared by a first-rate chef. A vegetable pizza was superb. My favorite dish was a mushroom entrée sautéed in a garlic sauce. It was so good, I had it two nights running. With dinner, I tried Lithuanian beer, which I found to be terrific. My favorite was a black beer whose name I forget—I doubt I could pronounce it, if I recalled it.

The restaurant in the hotel, and in all the restaurants we visited, had a tendency to play music excessively loud. This led to unusual aural experiences. The DJs are shouting about something or other in Lithuanian—for all I know, it could be Russian or Polish—and all of a sudden Bruce Springsteen is singing "Jersey Girl" in English. It comes as a pleasant, although unsettling, surprise, to have untranslated American rock on Lithuanian radio.

I didn't hear Danko, Fjeld, and Andersen, but there was Peter, Paul, and Mary *Blowin' in the Wind*. I heard this while in a pizzeria on Pilies St. I had ordered pizza with mushrooms—*funghi*, it said on the menu. It sounds better in English.

The Church of St. Michael is a brief walk from Pilies St. It was begun in 1594 and is finished as a church. It serves now as the Museum of Architecture. "Museum" is not the right word, since the exhibition amounts to a few display cases on the history of Vilnius. One can follow the progress of Vilnius from a medieval market town into a modern metropolis of half a million people. Archeological investigations have located settlements as old as two thousand years in Vilnius, but the origin of the city we know dates from the early fourteenth century when Duke Gediminas founded the city because of a dream. The original location of the fort founded by Gediminas stood close to the Cathedral and to Castle Hill. This site expanded over the centuries, so that today Vilnius is a sprawling city impossible to take by foot. In former days the city—town, rather—was surrounded by sturdy castle walls. Today, Vilnius is surrounded by Soviet-era high-rises, all strikingly alike, all strikingly drab. I don't know what the operative word in Lithuanian is, but in New Jersey we call such buildings "projects".

There is a small chapel in the right corner of St. Michael's. This chapel was probably enclosed when the church was functioning, but it stands bare now and exposed to the display cases. Along the wall in the chapel are thick bas-reliefs of Leo Sapiega and his family, the medieval lords who built the church and used it as a mausoleum, insofar as one can use a mausoleum for anything. There are mummified remains of the Sapiegas in the crypts below the church. For a few *litas* it is possible to view what's left of this once noble family. We didn't avail ourselves of the opportunity.

The most widely praised of all the churches in Vilnius stands a block from St. Michael's. This is the Church of St. Anne, located on Maironio *Gatve*. (Maironio was an early twentieth century Lithuanian poet. He's completely unknown to me, but then a lot of things are completely unknown to me. He's important enough to the Liths to be featured on the twenty *litas* note.) St. Anne's was founded in the sixteenth century and is considered to be the finest example of Gothic architecture in the country.

Napoleon passed through Vilnius on his way to Moscow in 1812. He was reported to have said, "I want to carry this church back to France on the palm of my hand." His statement refers to the beauty of the church and to its small size. It may also refer to the Emperor having an oversized hand.

The church does take some getting used to. We passed several times before we recognized it as the famous St. Anne's. The church is of small size, it's built of dark red and brown bricks, and there's no close vantage that can reveal its beauty in a single glance. The sidewalk in front of the main door is a few paces wide. You have to cross the street and walk a block in order to see the church from any expansive angle, and even then the view is obstructed by telephone lines and traffic signs.

What makes the church unique is the amount of architectural detail built into the walls. The center façade consists of a pair of convoluted turrets constructed around four tall and exceptionally narrow windows. These turrets twist about at roof level, forming an amazingly delicate pattern, as if the architect took strings of brick and looped a complex knot around four sticks of glass.

At first glance the design appeared flowery. But the design altered the longer I looked. It became, in outline, a kind of brow, where the bricks served for facial bones and the windows for eye slits. I had the impression a medieval presence hidden in the brick face was staring at me. The sensation wasn't frightening or creepy. Rather, it was somewhat sad and strangely solemn. I interpreted the presence as the genius of a holy place. It might even have been the genius of a very old country struggling to free itself from a brutal past. James Joyce wrote that "history is a nightmare from which we are trying to awaken." Penned about blood-soaked Erin, his words are as appropriate to *Lietuva*.

To the left of St. Anne's is a bell tower built of the same brick as the church. The tower dates to the late nineteenth century. It's on a much smaller scale than the towers outside the Cathedral and St. John's. Like the church, the tower is capped by an incredibly intricate peak.

The Church of the Bernardines stands directly behind St. Anne's, literally back-to-back with it. But this church is on a different scale, being perhaps three times as long and twice as tall. The exterior of the church is painted an appealing mix of white and pink. Like the churches we saw in Vilnius and in Turgeli, it has that peculiar brick extension rising over the façade. Only here the bricks rise much higher over roof level—it's like an erect tassel over a fez. I would hate to be under that tassel in a windstorm.

The Church of the Bernardines was established in the late sixteenth century. The building is one of the largest in the Old Town and has the thickest walls in any church I've ever seen. The walls look thicker for holding wonderfully tall windows. In fact, the church served on occasion as a fort and was the site of artillery duels in former times.

The church is a shell of its former self. It withstood centuries of war, but not the avarice of Soviet occupiers. There is a makeshift altar surrounded by a few rows of folding chairs. There are several candle racks and a rather abstract metallic icon of the Holy Spirit flies over the altar. To the left of the altar, on a brick pedestal, is a huge bell. And that is all.

The barren interior makes the church look even larger, and the beautifully fluted white pillars that connect the floor with the ceiling look as if they were carrying the sky. We walk along the side naves. The late afternoon light breaks our shadows on the backs of the folding chairs. In modern homes picture frames left on walls for too long leave their traces on the paint. Here, the old walls are imprinted with large rectangular stains. Probably, the imprints portrayed the Stations of the Cross, since they occur at regular intervals. If we inspected the walls close up, we probably could find nail marks.

There's an aphorism to the effect that attractive people have dull personalities and unattractive people possess character—I like to think that's the case. The aphorism also applies to churches. The Church of the Bernardines is bereft of artwork other than a squat bell and a futuristic sculpture flying above the altar. There's nothing to look at, other than the impressive emptiness. Sts. Peter and Paul, the Chapel of St. Casimir, the Chapel of the Black Madonna—they're too beautiful to be anything else than what they are. But this church—this church definitely has character. *Spirit* is a better term, *presence* better still. And I would say the presence is that of *waiting*.

Waiting for what, I can't say, but I can venture the guess that this church is waiting to learn if it will be repaired—and if Lithuania will be repaired. This church has witnessed so many turns and twists in the violent history of its country, it withholds judgment on a wild act of liberation. A closed society has become an open society—this church has seen societies close and open and close again. A repressive regime has been thrown aside—this church has seen repressive regimes come and go and come back again. Its massive presence has outlived dictatorships by the boatload. The signature bell has pealed on the deaths of tyrants, only to be struck by the next tyrant. The world goes blithely on and on, round and round from disaster to disaster, and this church, its fate intertwined with its country's, wisely prefers to wait than to sound hosannas prematurely.

The last evening of our stay we visited the historic television tower at the outskirts of Vilnius. This tower, the tallest structure in a flat land, is something like fifty stories high. There's a revolving restaurant at the top. It makes one revolution an hour. The elevators make one trip an hour; if you miss their arrival, you have to go round again. The base of the tower was the site of an attack by KGB troops on "Bloody Sunday", January 13, 1991. This event resulted in the deaths of thirteen civilians. Political extortion had grown bloody that day, and the violence had been caught on camera. Lithuania and the world saw that Soviet valentines were delivered by truncheons.

From the restaurant, you can see for miles. The brown Neris slices through a nearby park. The Hotel Lietuva is in the distance. The advertisement hasn't switched on, but the building is identifiable by its bulk. Behind it, but not visible, is the Naujasis Vilnius. Farther afield is the Old Town, easily mapped by the maze of amber tiles on the roofs. Beyond the Old Town extend swaths of green, hazy in strong sunlight. Somewhere in the green distance lie my ancestral towns.

We took trolley number nine when we left the television tower. I hope we didn't look too much like tourists. We wanted only to arrive safely at the hotel and to have dinner in the wonderful restaurant there. The ride wasn't eventful, but it was psychologically daunting, since we didn't pay for the trip. Riders buy tickets at kiosks along the route—although more tastefully constructed, such kiosks resemble the newspaper and candy booths in New York City subway stations—and punch them in a machine located on a pole in the trolley. There was no kiosk where we caught the trolley and the driver was secluded in a separate compartment from the riders and quite inaccessible. The fine for riding without a punched ticket was twenty *litas*—five American dollars. My concern that an international incident would break out when hard-faced men in trench coats stormed on board demanding, "Where are your punched tickets?" abated when the trolley became too crowded for the gendarmerie to inspect. I noted about halfway along that no one was punching tickets when they entered. The only exception was a churlish old lady who looked as if she wouldn't have minded having the Great Father drive.

Lithuania is a divided country. Vilnius is a modern metropolis of traffic, businesses, retail outlets, and people on the go. It's definitely a city of young people. This may be an exaggeration, but most of the old people we saw were either sitting in the parks or begging. Young women appear to have made the transition to capitalism more readily than young men, who generally wear ill-fitting fashions not seen in the West since *I Spy* went off the air. As a group, the women in Vilnius were among the most beautiful, and certainly the tallest, I have ever seen.

I think if we had visited two or three years earlier we would have observed an entirely different spirit, but it's hard to believe the Vilnius we saw endured two World Wars and forty years of Soviet stupefaction. I came away with a clear sense that the people know perfectly well what they are moving toward—it's called "the almighty dollar". I suppose I have to say "the almighty *lita*", although I'm not sure how mighty the *lita* will turn out to be.

It's an entirely different situation in the countryside. Physically, the land south of Vilnius takes travelers back a century. Horses used as tractors, woodpiles the height of barns, hand-held implements, backbreaking labor, sustenance farming, outhouses—we could have visited in 1897 as in 1997. The people we met in Kalniskes and Girdziunai know they're not going back to collective farming and they hope they're not going back to a police state. But they have no conception what they are moving toward. The almighty dollar doesn't flash as freely in their regions as in the capital.

There's a feeling—this is stronger in Kalniskes than in Girdziunai—that the government hasn't played fair with the people. The president is only for the rich. The police can be trusted only when they are bribed. Bureaucrats take advantage of their positions. Wealthy people grab land in unscrupulous ways. The infrastructure is falling apart. Roads no longer exist, jobs no longer exist, markets no longer exist. Lithuanian politicians ape their Soviet mentors and punish people of Polish ethnicity—there is a serious ethnic rift between Balts and Slavs in Southeastern Lithuania. Poisons from the Ukraine ride the wind and cause obscure diseases. There is no one to turn to, there is no help to be gotten. The situation does not look good.

I hope things work out for my Bielawski and Storta cousins. I have a sense the latter will adapt better. They seem to have more to start with, a higher socioeconomic level, as it were, and they may have more progressive genes. I heard that my grandmother was more modern and forward-looking than my grandfather. What may have been true in New Jersey in the 1920s may be true in Lithuania in the 1990s.

Both families are *decent* people, and that was a gratifying genealogical finding. The most uncertain part of the trip, once we got off the propeller plane, was wondering what kind of relatives we had, we knew not of. After all, they could have been the local *nomenklatura*, or the local lawless authorities, or, literally, the local horse thieves. It was a pleasure to learn that the decency

I see in my mother and in my American relatives exists overseas in cousins exposed to entirely different, and more difficult, circumstances. It made me feel very good about myself.

So, I raise my glass of black beer and salute *Lietuva*, its people, its land, its future. And I salute our Bielawski ancestors of Kalniskes, and our Storta ancestors of Girdziunai, and all the people across the world descended from these families.

RETURN TO THE AMBER COUNTRY

Lithuania—June, 2000

June 6

Our trip was made on Scandinavian Airlines from Newark via Stockholm to Vilnius on the way out and from Vilnius to Newark via Copenhagen on the way home. The flight to Lithuania was not easy. The plane was crowded, the engines were exceptionally noisy, and two rude ladies sitting in front of us insisted on reclining as far as the swivels took them. This left us sitting in what were effectively phone booths. It was hard to get to sleep under these conditions, although I'm not sure whether the noise or the crowding or the cramping was responsible—or whether sleep in an erect posture was possible under any condition.

The flight on the way home was equally uncomfortable. The plane was crowded, the engines were noisy, and the passengers sitting in front of us were as rude as the ladies on the flight out. And, flying westward, we had the sun the entire trip. It's disconcerting to read 10:00 PM and 11:00 PM and midnight on the wristwatch and see the bright, blazing sunlight. The sun held steady in the sky hour after hour after brutal hour. It didn't set until we were two hours out of Newark—this was something like 5:00 AM on our watches.

In one of his works Mark Twain promised never to mention the weather. (Basil Fawlty promised never to mention the war.) I'll get it over with and mention the weather—I doubt I can mention the weather just one time. The first two days of our visit were wet and rainy. The middle two were overcast and damp. The last two were sunny and hot, which means temperatures in the eighties.

Our Lithuanian connection didn't show at the Vilnius Airport. (He failed to show in 1997, as well. This year, we got a refund.) After some haggling over prices—one driver actually wanted forty-five *litas*— we settled on a cab for twenty-three *litas*. With a tip of two *litas*, the ride cost five American dollars, which is less than we would spend going in a cab around a block in Manhattan.

The Hotel Naujasis Vilnius, a four-star hotel now, has changed for the better since our first trip. Our room (#510) was much larger than what we had in 1997. The view from the window was far superior compared to 1997 when we had only the Hotel Lietuva to contemplate. We can see the top of the Cathedral from the hotel room. Behind the Cathedral, the topmost portion of Gediminas Tower on Castle Hill is visible. At night the Tower is illuminated—it's like a harvest moon in brick. The silver dome of the Planetarium on Snipiskiu *Gatve* is a block away. Beyond the Planetarium the distinguished steeples of the Church of St. Raphael conceal a large portion of the city from view.

The room has a color television with a remote control, which is quite unlike 1997. There are approximately twenty stations. Three are in English— CNN (showing mostly soccer previews), a travel network (showing mostly documentaries about African safaris), and a cartoon network (showing mostly cartoons).

The plane left Newark at 5:45 PM on Monday, June 5. We arrived at the hotel at noon on Tuesday. After a short rest, we strolled across the Green Bridge, which crosses the Neris River, to Gedimino *Gatve* and to the Cathedral. What familiar sites! The muscular bronze statues on the bridge, built to glorify Soviet workers in the heyday of communism. The great black bulk of the Opera House on the right. Children splash in the three levels of fountains. The tiny park on the left side of the street, where the crowds wait for the buses and the trolleys. In the park elderly ladies quietly sell bouquets. The yellow slab of the former Communist Party Headquarters is to the left of the park. McDonald's is to the right, next to the university bookstore.

Young people lounge at the outdoor tables, eating Big Macs and drinking Kalnapilis beer. We're four thousand miles from Jersey City, but there's a strange feeling of familiarity. It's like a feeling of coming home.

A large section of the plaza in front of the Cathedral, including the bell tower, is inaccessible owing to renovation projects. Huge black and gray slabs are being laid down as pavement. The project is controversial, since the country is poor and the slabs, which were made in China, cost millions. There's a hint of political corruption because of cost overruns. I don't feel like we left Hudson County at all.

Dressed in canvas and scaffolding, the buildings across the street from the Cathedral are also inaccessible. One of the buildings held the Literary Salon, the restaurant from which Czeslaw Milosz viewed the Red Army take over Vilnius. The restaurant is closed, I don't know whether permanently or temporarily. Its closing is disappointing, since it afforded a great view of the Cathedral and was graced with a unique ambiance of history and literature. The food wasn't bad either.

There are large-scale archeological explorations going on immediately behind the Cathedral, in the park between it and Gediminas Tower on the great hill. Excavations are also going on atop the hill. This area is the oldest part of the city of Vilnius, formally dating from the thirteenth century and earlier. Until recently, very little archeology was done to explore the area. This kind of investigation would have been impossible in Soviet times, when the last thing the government wanted was for people to take pride in their ethnic past.

The present Cathedral, the sixth on the site, dates from 1783-1801. The architect was Laurynas Gucevicius, who died before its completion. The building is in the classical style. The interior design is a simple Gothic pattern of a huge central nave with narrow side naves. There are a number of enclosed chapels along the exterior walls, the most famous and beautiful one being the Chapel of St. Casimir. The Cathedral was closed when atheism became the state religion in communist times. Pope John Paul II visited in September, 1993.

The bell tower that stands in front of the Cathedral is one of the oldest structures in Vilnius. The bottom story was a defensive tower built at the end of the fourteenth century. It connects to a still older stone wall now buried below street level. The upper three stories have been added across the centuries. The tower has been in its present form for two hundred years. Time has been kept more or less accurately.

The Cathedral is very impressive from the exterior—it's a gigantic white building a city-block long and decorated with oversized statues of disagreeable-looking saints. Atop the building are restorations of the statues of Saints Stanislaw (holding a silver cross), Helen, and Casimir. The originals stood for more than a century when the communists destroyed them in 1950. Near the corners of the front walls are statues of St. John the Beloved and Moses (with horns). Somewhat smaller versions of the four evangelists stand among Old Testament figures. A relief called "Noah's Offering" is at the crown of the building.

The interior of the Cathedral is not as impressive as the exterior—and it's not as impressive as I remember. The building is immense—there are huge square columns holding the ceiling in place and the sky above it. But the floor plan is modest and the artwork is sparse. Sparse, that is, if we overlook the amazing Chapel of St. Casimir.

Simple wood pews lead to a monumental, but strangely bland, high altar. A grandfather clock stands near the main altar. The pendulum can be seen swinging from the entrance. I'm not sure of the historical significance of the clock or of its spiritual significance. It lends an austere, library-like quality to the interior.

I've noticed that many of the churches in Lithuania are ponderous on the exterior, but cramped and cozy in the interior. I wonder if this disparity may be due to the fact that the churches served other functions in olden times—they may have been forts and places of refuge. And the churches in the countryside may have doubled as market places and public spaces for meetings. I'm almost tempted to say that this disparity was the original plan. God's house should appear monumental from the outside, so that we feel small and insignificant, but when we are inside we should feel an intimacy and closeness with the Lord. This conjecture sounds good, but it requires a lot more knowledge of religion and architecture than I possess, and most of these churches have undergone considerable alterations in the twentieth century. It may be that the disparity between loud exteriors and soft interiors relates more to accidents of history than to any coherent plan of priest or architect.

St. Stanislaw, for whom the Cathedral is named, is the patron saint of Poland. He was born near Cracow in July, 1030. Although born into royalty, he forsook wealth for the church, rising to the rank of bishop. He came into conflict with King Boleslaw II of Poland, who he excommunicated. In May, 1079, he was slain while saying mass, which guarantees admission into heaven with no stops along the way. He was canonized in 1253 and is buried in Cracow.

There's a second St. Stanislaw. This is St. Stanislaw Kostka, who is an interesting personage. This saint was born in Poland in 1550. He tried to enter the Jesuit order, but was rejected on account of his youth. This inspired him to walk five hundred miles to Germany, where St. Peter Canisius directed him to Rome. After another long walk, he entered a seminary there, only to die in 1568. He is the patron saint of young people and of people suffering doubts, which should have made him universally venerated.

After our brief visit to the Cathedral, we dined outdoors at the Vidudienis restaurant on Gedimino *Gatve*. Babci had ravioli in a butter sauce and I had a delicious black bean and scallion salad followed by pizza. The pizza was made in a different style than what we're accustomed to in the States. The crust was very thin and slices of *pomidor*—tomato—floated in sauce under a thin layer of cheese. I also enjoyed my first Lithuanian beer in three years.

I never understood why the Lithuanians don't export their beer—the main labels are Utenos, Fortus, and Kalnapilis—or, at the minimum, advertise to get them better known. The brands I sampled have a rich flavor, not at all bitter. I haven't majored in beer drinking—brandy is my forte—but I think Lithuanian beer tastes better than American, Irish, and German beers.

Lithuanian coffee is stronger than American coffee, but Maxwell House need not worry about competition in this department. Lithuanian coffee, whether served in restaurants or in private homes, is awful, being thick and bitter to the taste. It's like instant coffee used to taste decades ago. Coffee at McDonald's tastes better—but this is damning with washed-out grinds.

It's possible to trace Lithuanian history by the names of Gedimino *Gatve*, the main street in Vilnius. The presidential palace and parliament building are at the western end, maybe a mile distant. The Cathedral anchors the eastern end. In Tsarist times the avenue was called George *Gatve*, whoever George was. When the Poles captured Vilnius in the 1920s the avenue was renamed Adam Mickiewicz *Gatve*, after the illustrious poet. It was renamed Lenin *Gatve* in the first Soviet occupation. It became Gedimino *Gatve* when the Nazis stormed into town. When the Soviets returned in 1944, it became Stalin *Gatve*. After The Great Father died and fell out of favor, it reverted to Lenin *Gatve*. When Lithuania became independent in 1991 the name reverted to Gedimino.

If history's any guide, it'll stay Gedimino *Gatve* until the next invasion.

I observed fewer beggars than in 1997. There was only one lady kneeling at the entrance of St. Raphael's. Babci thinks it was the same unfortunate who was there in 1997, but my memory's not as good. There were two beggars at the entrance of the Cathedral; one looked to be psychologically disordered.

People beg in the same self-effacing manner I remembered from our first trip. The women tend to sit on the ground. The men stand with caps doffed. They never catch your eye and they speak only when they receive alms. They also bow profusely. A few *litas* can go a long way in this country—let's hope they go as far in purgatory, where they may be able to shed a few decades off the purifying fires.

Vilnius is a city of young people—or Gedimino *Gatve* is. Young people are everywhere. The young women—tall and thin and beautiful—dress in the height of current fashion. Baltic women look as if they belong on the covers of magazines. The young men, also tall and thin and not so beautiful, are not as well dressed. Kids are everywhere, eight-and-ten-year-olds running and skating and biking through the heart of the city. The kids look like American kids, with tee shirts emblazoned with rock icons. They also act like American kids, except that they're more polite.

I may have missed them, myself being permanently young at heart, but there didn't seem to be any middle-aged people about, other than beggars and the tourist trade. An occasional senior citizen hobbles past. Sometimes, the seniors stumble on by banging a walking stick on the pavement. This sends shivers upward, considering what these people have been through in a century of occupying armies.

I'm not suggesting conspiracy, but the question presents itself—where is everyone between the ages of forty and eighty? If I ignore the possibility that they've been ground up and served in the local restaurants, the answer is obvious. The middle-aged people have either been excluded, or have excluded themselves, from the march of progress. They don't visit the upscale Old Town or the upscale business district. They can't afford to. They don't feel they belong or have a part in the transformation of a closed society. They're not sure the new society wants them or whether they want it. They stay at home in the outlying districts or on their farms and they suffer resentment over where their society is going—without them. This is sad, considering the age segregation and the failed opportunities. It's also understandable. The future has always been with the young, never more than in times of traumatic change.

Observing all the young people on Gedimino *Gatve*, observing how good they look and how fast they walk and how confident and assertive they behave, I feel sure that this society is not going backward into the mortifying totalitarianism of the past.

Tuesday's highlight was the surprise visit of Wladyslawa Kucsynska, Babci's second cousin, at the hotel around 7:30 PM. Wladyslawa, who is descended from Matweg Storta, is a tall lady of about fifty years. She has gray-black hair and a ruddy complexion. She resides in Vilnius three days a week, where she teaches preschool. In Vilnius, she is studying Lithuanian, which is being adopted as the official language in the education system. The rest of the week she is in Dieveniskes, where she resides and where we will visit in three days. Dieveniskes is about fifty miles to the south. She travels back and forth by bus.

Our conversation was generic—about family, children, school, Vilnius, and New York. It was difficult to communicate, since Wladyslawa speaks no English and we speak the Jersey City dialect of Polish. I speak a dialect of Polish that has never been heard on this planet. But I think we showed we were decent people and Wladyslawa showed social graces, bringing us candies and declining our offer of a late coffee. (We made plans for the following evening.) Throughout the visit, Wladyslawa wore a pleasant smile, perhaps because of my attempt to speak Polish, a *trudny younzekka* or "difficult language" in the kind of accented English I speak.

Wladyslawa thought Babci looked like the Storta side of the family, which was an interesting observation, coming from an informed source.

June 7

A wonderful day of family history!

We met our guide, Emilia P—, and our driver, Kestas, who we remembered from three years ago. Emilia is a thin middle-aged lady with black hair. She guides tourists on the side. Her main job is in the hotel industry.

Emilia was more political than Irena, our guide in 1997. She was very proud of Lithuania, but not particularly proud of the present administration, who she felt was incompetent and corrupt. She believed the government was not responsive to the needs of the citizens and that it was failing to create a middle class. She thought this was the secret of success in the United States, that a consumer-rich and politically-active middle class had developed. She said that in Lithuania there were only two classes—the very rich and the very poor.

On our three tours she inquired about the language capabilities of our hosts and was quite vocal in encouraging them to learn Lithuanian. She observed that Mecislav and Viktor Bielawski couldn't read a menu in a restaurant in Vilnius, since they speak only Polish and the menus are in Lithuanian and, thank the God of chefs, in English. And she believed their inability to speak Lithuanian prevented them from finding better jobs.

There's an undercurrent of ethnic conflict in Southeastern Lithuania. The Lithuanians have been history's fools for centuries, having been dominated by Poland, Germany, and Russia at various times. Part of this domination, especially with the Russians since the start of the nineteenth century, involved the attempt to purge Lithuanian culture and to suppress the language. Since 1991 ethnic Lithuanians have been in power and they are regurgitating the resentment built up over the centuries. I doubt the conflict will spill over into violence, since every group in this region had been equally bullied by the Russians, but the conflict is real and is being waged on linguistic and cultural battlefronts.

Emilia expressed considerable bitterness over the Soviet regime, claiming it sapped the will of the people and squelched initiative. She claimed a hangover of the Soviet era persisted in that many people in Lithuania do the absolute minimum in any job. However, she praised the concept of a "collective farm", since it better utilized the resources of poverty-stricken communities. She felt that individual small farmers could not succeed without pooling their resources.

And she was very much down on alcoholism. She belittled three tipsy young people we stopped for directions and she made disparaging remarks about two men who were seated on a curb in Dieveniskes. In the former case she attributed alcoholism to the 30% rate of unemployment in the rural area. In the latter case her ire was aroused by the fact that the men were publicly passing a bottle back-and-forth.

The only other case of public drunkenness I experienced was in the Old Town in Vilnius, when an one-eyed elderly gent, obviously in his cups, laid the glad hand on me.

After a few wrong turns we found Malakonys *kaimas*, where my great-grandmother, Ursula Milosz, was born. This is a tiny village a few miles to the southwest of Turgeli, the parish town. Of course, there really isn't a "village" of Malakonys, as we understand the term. The place is merely a group of badly kept houses arranged on high ground at an intersection of roads. I saw approximately ten houses; probably, there were additional houses off the road. And they really aren't "roads", as we understand the term. The roads are merely gravel paths overgrown with grass and deeply rutted in places.

Despite being closer to civilization, as we understand the word, Malakonys looked in poorer repair than Girdziunai. The houses were dilapidated and none that I saw was painted. Hens ran everywhere and a truck with a cow inside pulled up as we arrived. Nothing in the surrounding countryside looked to be under cultivation other than small vegetable gardens at the sides of the houses.

Emilia asked a tall young lady tending one of these gardens if she knew anyone by the family name of Milosz. The young lady replied that her mother was named Milosz and that she would run to get her mother. Which she did on the instant, leaving a toddler to cry insistently for "Mama".

Presently, two middle-aged ladies appeared, one of whom was the mother. We started to make inquiries, when they said they would get their father. Which they did on the instant. They returned with a gentleman of eighty-nine years. Which he looked. He was short and somewhat stocky. He had bright blue eyes and thick white hair. He walked with a cane and his right arm shook dramatically.

This man was the last surviving child of Martynas Milosz, son of Motiejus Milosz and Marijona Satkewicz. Motiejus was my great-grandmother's older brother, which means we were in the same family group. He didn't remember hearing about Ursula, for the understandable reason that she died in 1889, but he knew the Bielawski family of Kalniskes.

According to the old man, Martynas sired eight children. He died around 1934.

The old man—we never knew his name—was aware of an uncle, Antanas, who was the son of Kazimier Milosz and Viktorija Vilkinis. (Kazimier was another brother of Ursula.) He told us Antanas died before Martynas— around 1930—and had three sons and two daughters, one of whom was alive.

We showed the notes I had prepared on the Milosz family, but neither the elderly man nor the ladies knew much. One of my objectives was to push our Milosz ancestry to the 1820s. Despite the poverty and the awful history of this place, church records are extant for the peasantry that far back. There are two possible origins for the Milosz line in that period, but these people had no information beyond the names of their fathers and uncles. In fact, I had far more information than they had—this has been the case throughout our genealogical researches. For the most part the people who resided in the ancestral villages had little knowledge beyond their immediate families.

Malakonys was a moving experience. The last recorded citation for Martynas Milosz in the records I've accumulated was made in 1900, when he served as a godparent to one of my grandfather's half-brothers. A century later, and after a trip of four thousand miles concluding in a thoroughly obscure place, we got to meet the last surviving child of Martynas. This is truly a connection across time and space.

Before we took our leave, the old man's daughter informed us that we had come at a fortunate time, since it was her father's birthday. Well, it was his lucky day, after all. We gave him a present of twenty *litas*, along with a chorus of *sto lats*, which is Polish for "one-hundred years".

We left Malakonys for Kalniskes, which is a few miles and five minutes drive to the south. Kalniskes is not as centralized as Malakonys or Girdziunai. The houses are scattered and separated from each other by thick clumps of foliage. A few houses sit on elevations. An awful road—a sandwich of dirt and tall grass—twists and turns in amazing angles as it wanders from house to house. Michail Bielawski's house appears to be at the end of the road.

We approached the house from a different direction than the one we took three years ago. That year, Kestas merely drove across a grassy field. Our entrance was on the road this year, so it was more dignified, but no less bumpy.

The Bielawski homestead has improved since our last visit. Two additional sheds or small barns have been added. We learned later that Michail's sons built the new buildings. The large woodshed, which I remembered from our previous visit, was well stocked. As before, hens scurried about. A car was parked near the house; this was certainly new. On our last visit they had access to a motorcycle.

The interior of the house was unchanged. We were ushered into the living room. This is a makeshift room formed by the exterior walls of the building and by the strategic placement of cabinets and a curtain. The doors to both the front door and to the living room were closed behind us. At first, I thought this might have had to do with security, but I learned it was to keep flies out.

A generous meal was prepared—various types of fatty pork, tomatoes and cucumbers, potatoes, meatballs and noodles, homemade bread, the requisite kielbasa, and several types of liquor. No matter that our hosts were poor— they respected the ancient virtue of hospitality.

Michail has aged since our previous visit. His hair, which is cut close, has turned mostly grayish white. And his face has reddened considerably. He is sixty years of age.

Helena, his wife, is as lovely and lively as ever. She stands maybe four-foot-nine and weighs maybe ninety pounds with bricks in her side pockets, but she has the personality of a much larger person. She exhibited a frenetic level of activity throughout our stay. It started with her running up to the van and hugging us energetically and it never slowed down.

We heard a wonderful story about Helena. The night before our arrival she baked a babka in honor of our visit. A thunderstorm broke out while she was baking. She became so frightened of the storm, she forgot to ice the babka.

Marija Dashevic, Michail's sister, and her husband Stanislaw, joined us for dinner. Marija, who is sixty one, is slightly taller than Michail— everyone is slightly taller than Michail—and resembles him facially. She has black and gray hair and, like Babci and Michail, the distinctive Bielawski nose. Wladyslawa claimed Babci took after the Storta side, but I think the resemblance to the Bielawski side is greater.

Neither Marija nor Stanislaw said much during our visit. They looked like pleasant people, since they smiled throughout. Their smiles couldn't be because of my distinctive Polish, since Emilia did the talking.

Mecislav and Viktor, Michail's sons, have both matured since our last visit. Mecislav is now twenty eight and Viktor is now twenty one. Both have found work and both have experienced problems collecting pay. Viktor has not been paid a full salary in something like seven months. In Mecislav's case employees got paid only when they threatened the manager with physical harm. The problem of collecting the fruits of one's wages is endemic in satellites of the former Soviet Union. There's either no regard for employee rights or companies fail and everyone gets stuck. I inquired about their obtaining political or legal assistance, as we would in the United States, but they dismissed this possibility. There is no one to complain to. They have no connection with the political process and they have no extra money to fight to get their rightful wages.

Mecislav is marrying in Vilnius in July. His bride works in the bakery business. However, there is sadness, since his prospective mother-in-law is ill with cancer and may not survive until the wedding.

We were joined later in the day by Bronislawa, the daughter of Felix Bielawski, my grandfather's half-brother. Bronislawa is about sixty years of age. Her face is more rounded and more lined than her cousins'. Her gray hair is cut short. She lives in Kalniskes.

We learned that Felix died in 1978 and is buried in Turgeli cemetery. There's longevity somewhere in the line, since Felix would have been in his mid-eighties when he died and his sister, Juzufa, is still alive at ninety.

They told us that Michail Bielawski, my great-grandfather, worked very hard under difficult social and political circumstances to save Russian money to send his sons to America. They said that Josef came over first and then my grandfather Pawel, but this is not what our records indicate. They repeated what they told us last time, that Jonas, their father, was not permitted to emigrate owing to some problem with his lungs.

Michail and his family, knowing that we wanted to visit some local spots, drove ahead of us as we left their farm. They stopped about a mile from their house and indicated that the field to our left was the location of the farm where Michail and Ursula lived in the nineteenth century and where my grandfather and his brothers were born. I took quite a few pictures of the place and hurried to find a rock to grab as a memento. It had started to rain and all the rocks had gone underground. Incredibly, there wasn't so much as a pebble to be found.

The field was bereft of human habitation or of any obvious trace that anyone had lived there. Of course, everything would have been of perishable wood. A row of trees, located perhaps twenty or so yards from the road, stretched in a precise line. This could have been the remnants of an orchard, since the file looked too precise to have grown by chance. Another row of trees was closer to the road, but these were haphazardly arranged by Mother Nature.

I concentrated on the orchard-like arrangement, but Bronislawa rushed forward and pointed in the opposite direction to a large shrub located in a clump of trees. I guessed this spot must have been the exact place, so I took photographs and continued my search for rocks. Unfortunately, they were no more plenteous than on the road. I managed to find one tiny specimen that came home with us to New Jersey.

We next traveled to Zaltuny Cemetery—but there is no longer any cemetery at Zaltuny. It's merely a field alongside the road that leads to Turgeli. There is an interesting story about this cemetery. Learning it, and having come from the field where our Bielawski ancestors lived, I felt as if I were uncovering a chunk of lost history.

The cemetery had been unused for a long time, maybe a hundred years. Whatever upkeep was performed on the grounds would have ceased when the last of the families of the interred stopped visiting. Most of the crosses would have been of wood and long since disintegrated. From the 1940s the cemetery grounds were used as pasture for cattle. A creamery collective had been built next to the pastureland. The creamery was in operation until the fall of communism, when it, too, fell into ruins.

Mecislav informed us that a headstone stood somewhere in the grass. It was the only symbol that the field once held human graves. Despite the rain, we left the cars and searched for this stone. We followed the road about halfway to the ruins of the creamery, then stepped across a narrow drainage trough. After a few minutes, Mecislav located the stone.

It was a flat gray headstone about three feet tall and rather heavy looking. A much smaller stone, black in color and flattened, was to the left. A cross was at the top of the large stone. The letters "J.M." and the year "1875" were chiseled below the cross. The small stone had no decipherable writing.

Both stones were too bulky—and too full of bad luck—to grab as mementoes.

We continued onto Turgeli cemetery and viewed the graves of Felix Bielawski and his wife and of Kotryna Bielawska, Michail's mother. It was fortunate Michail came along, as we could never have found these graves on our own.

The cemetery is located behind the Church of the Virgin Mary. It's an incredibly crowded and cluttered place, with innumerable family plots enclosed inside metal railings and with a bewildering variety of monuments. The latter defy description. Some monuments are spare crosses, often of wood, others are huge headstones, with fancy carvings and tiny windows in which photographs of the deceased stare at visitors. The plots themselves vary greatly in upkeep. Some are beautifully cared for, with elaborate floral displays; some have benches enclosed. Other plots haven't been tended in years; in these, the tall grass hides the names of the departed.

The cemetery is a dreary, depressing place reeking of mortality. We visited in pouring rain, but it was more than the rain. The ground was uneven and raised in places, so there was an eerie sensation that we were standing at the center of a pit surrounded by graves.

Besides the diversity of monuments, there is another unusual aspect about the graves that I haven't seen in American cemeteries. Spouses are often buried side-by-side rather than in the same grave. Frequently, there are separate headstones—and these can be quite different in style when the spouses die in different periods. Michail's parents demonstrated this aspect of burials. His mother's grave is clearly marked, but Jonas's grave has been lost. It's somewhere nearby, maybe even to the side, but no one is sure. Kotryna wanted her children to remember where their father's grave was, but they lost its place. This failure is understandable, given the wide difference in dates of death—Jonas died in 1946, Kotryna in 1982—and the dearth of records.

It was at the entrance of the cemetery that we took leave of Michail and his family. Who knows whether we shall see these fine people again?

Neither the day nor family history were over yet.

We were paged by the hotel that we had a visitor—Gintautas Pupalaigis, the son of Marija, who we will visit tomorrow. Gintautas looks better than his name. He's a slim, light-haired fellow of about thirty five. He was on the way with his son to a rock concert in the nearby stadium—they were going to see the group Eight Inch Nails—and stopped to inquire how we would travel to Salcininki. After a bit of confusion, we made it plain we had arranged for a driver and translator. (Gintautas speaks a little English, which can lead to more confusion than if he spoke no English; his English accent is as bad as my Polish accent.) He's an educated person and a professional, unlike Michail's sons, who are farmers and laborers.

Later that evening we met Wladyslawa for dinner in the hotel. Babci had pork chops with fries and vegetables. I had a radish salad with scallions and sour cream followed by boiled vegetables.

Wladyslawa helped with our Storta ancestry. She informed us that her grandmother was Paulina Tuchovcha—she was the wife of Matweg Storta, who had immigrated to Jersey City in 1910 and who facilitated the marriage of his sister, Zofia, to Pawel Bielawski. Paulina was born around 1900 and died in 1990, having survived Matweg by an incredible fifty-six years. (She was around fifteen years younger than he was.)

Wladyslawa informed us that I had misrecorded the name of one of Matweg's siblings. The name was not *Josef,* as I thought, but *Juzufa*. She didn't know much about Juzufa's life, except to say that she died young. We later learned that Juzufa worked for the church, perhaps as a maid in a rectory.

And Wladyslawa suggested that our family was not related to a group of Storta families once located in the village of Dobralawny. This village is only a few miles from Girdziunai, the ancestral home of our Storta line. I was interested in the Dobralawny group because of the proximity of villages and because several of the latter settled in Bayonne, New Jersey, only a few miles from where the Stortas lived in Jersey City. The surname Storta is so uncommon in Lithuania and in America that a connection must exist between these family groups. The connection must be an old one, probably dating to the start of the nineteenth century or earlier.

After a pleasant hour of conversation we walked Wladyslawa to the bus stop. It was raining slightly, but we waited until she made her connection.

June 8

Another wonderful day of family history.

Emilia and Kestas called promptly at 10:00 AM and we commenced the ride to Salcininki. The terrain was familiar from our previous drives southward. The outskirts of Vilnius lie on steep hills, but the land south of the capital becomes very flat, with expansive fields and farms separated from each other by thick copses of trees and shrubbery. The farms shrank and the forest grew more dense the father south we proceeded.

We entered Salcininki from the north. The road continues straight through to the border with Belarus, which is only a few miles away. Halfway into town, a left turns takes you to Dieveniskes, our destination for tomorrow. Dieveniskes and Girdziunai are in that inexplicable Lithuanian peninsula that protrudes into Belarus.

We passed two *bankus* on the left side of the road. One has failed and gone out of business. This bank was in an attractive building with an ornate columned façade. The windows are boarded up.

The municipal building is on the right. This is an unremarkable glass structure dating from the Soviet era. Most of the buildings in Salcininki date from the Soviet era, which explains the dismal ambiance. (The area was the scene of fighting in WWII, so many of the older buildings were damaged or destroyed.) There's a statue of the poet Adam Mickiewicz outside the municipal building. The story is that he used to pass through Salcininki on his way to visit a girlfriend in a village presently located in Belarus. The connection with Salcininki is tenuous, but it's nice that a municipality honors a poet rather than a politician or a military officer.

Adam Mickiewicz is the leading literary personage in Lithuania, as he is in Poland and in Belarus—since his ancestry is unknown, all three nations claim him as their own. Mickiewicz was born in 1798 and died in Constantinople in 1855 while trying to form a Polish brigade to fight in the Crimean War. His early career was spent traveling throughout Europe espousing a number of controversial patriotic and religious causes. Mickiewicz wrote some of the most influential poems in the Polish language. His most famous works are *Grazyna* and *Pan Tadeusz*, both epics celebrating the peasant life. He originated the concept of Poland as the "Christ of nations", a theme which figures throughout his writings.

Salcininki is the regional center in this part of Lithuania, but it is a small place, numbering around eight thousand people. The houses are mostly single story and drab, most of them of wood. Grass and shrubbery grow on the sidewalks. There's a yellowish glow about the place, probably originating from the paint peeling from the bungalows on the main road.

Marija Pupalaigiene lives in a four-story apartment complex. The buildings are arranged to form a quadrangle, with a little room for parking, less for a lawn. The stairway inside is bleak, stone, and dirty—add graffiti and the buildings could stand as "projects" in Jersey City or Hoboken. Emilia informed us that there are no janitors or caretakers in such complexes and that tenants take responsibility only for their own apartments.

This was true in Marija's case. Her apartment is clean, airy, and tastefully decorated. The furniture is modern, although rather low—I felt as if I was sitting on the floor. There are two bathrooms and a balcony. A glass-enclosed bookcase stands next to the balcony. I perused the titles, but the books were in a foreign language.

I noticed that Marija's living room held few personal photographs or mementoes on the walls. I wonder if this is the custom in Lithuania, since Michail's living room also lacked personal touches and Danislav's had only two photographs on the wall—they might have put them up for our visit. Michail's walls held two icons of the Madonna, and Marija's had a large picture of the Risen Christ. But there were no pictures of the kids or grand-kids, as we would find in American homes.

Marija is a tall lady of sixty three, with light hair and squarish features. Her children are Irena, who, unfortunately, could not join us, and Gintautas, who we met yesterday. Gintautas works for the customs bureau in Vilnius. He took the day off so he could visit with us, but received a business call during dinner. He informed us that customs intercepted Americans in the

Vilnius airport attempting to transport guns. I got off a joke about Americans mistaking Vilnius for Dublin.

The highlight of our visit was meeting Juzufa Kozlowska, my mother's half-aunt, who lives with Marija. Juzufa is ninety years of age. She is slightly built, with gray hair pushed back. She has a dark complexion—I suppose this is what it looks like to be wizened—and the Bielawski nose that runs in that side of the family.

I joked that this is how Babci will look when she reaches ninety—the resemblance is definitely there.

Marija bragged that her mother was capable of walking to the market on her own, but Juzufa looked frail. She walks slowly and is hard of hearing. I wasn't sure that she fully knew who we were or what we were interested in. She stayed with us for a few brief intervals, periodically retiring to her bedroom. Twice, she returned with photographs of her family. There were a lot of pictures of marriages of her grandchildren, but few of olden times. Juzufa was orphaned at a young age, her father—my great-grandfather—dying when she was six, her mother when she was a teen. She had heard of my grandfather, but had little information about events before she was born. And she had lived through very difficult times. The luxuries of preserving mementoes of family history would have taken second place to personal survival.

It was wonderful meeting Juzufa, since she was living history—and a tenuous link with our living family history. I thought how important it would be for Marija or Gintautas to record her memories of the twentieth century, but it would have been impolite to broach this possibility.

After dinner—another fine spread—Gintautas took us on a tour of Salcininki and its surroundings. The region is a mixture of plains, heavy forest, and a number of long and narrow lakes, some of them artificial and stocked as fish farms. The lake region, which borders Belarus, appears devoid of villages. The few houses we saw were far and in between.

The region south of Salcininki was the scene of fierce guerilla fighting in the Nazi and communist periods. The Nazis razed several villages in the area, which may explain the low population. Modern rumors say that the communists were responsible for the disappearance of some of the villages. Mention of these rumors touched a sore spot, since no one, including the patriotic Emilia, was willing to elaborate. There must be many unexamined events from the communist period festering at the checkpoints of consciousness.

Marija keeps a summer cottage near one of the lakes. The place is accessible by a weed of a road that crosses between two lakes. The cottage, which is quite rustic and cozy, has four rooms, a huge fireplace, and a half-completed sauna. Next to the house is a vegetable garden that Marija personally tends.

We then returned to Salcininki and to a tour of the city. The language difficulties Emilia referred to were evident. Despite the tiny population, there are three separate grammar schools, one in Lithuanian, one in Russian, and the last and most populous in Polish. At some point going forward in the new century the three are supposed to be consolidated into a single Lithuanian school.

We passed a number of vacant city blocks set aside as private gardens. Each apartment in the housing complexes comes with a plot of land on which residents can grow vegetables. (Shades of the Irish rundale!) Gintautas informed us that some people keep cows on their plots, but we didn't see any loitering on public property. For that matter, we didn't see anyone tending the plots, but we drove by in the middle of the afternoon. I compared Marija's apartment with the "projects" in New Jersey, but the custom of including individually kept gardens on public land is light years removed from what we find in the Garden State.

The hospital where Danislav Storta's daughter works is a small building in the southern district of the city. The building resembles a factory or a truck depot more than a hospital. A failed sports arena is across the street from the hospital; the building has been recycled as a flea market.

Marija knew Danislav's daughter, who treated Juzufa at one point. Truly, it's a small world.

There's a legend in these parts how sickness came into the world. During the act of creation God made clay puppets or models of the original people before he turned them into flesh and blood. God set down his work before the clay hardened and stepped away for a moment. Satan sneaked into the work shed and poked holes in the puppets, disguising the spaces by stretching the clay. When God returned and made the clay into living flesh, the concealed holes, weak places from the get-go, were part of the finished product. The holes are the places where sicknesses lie in wait. This is a wonderfully vivid folktale and it bears some resemblance—I admit this is a stretch—to the genetic theory of illness. Both the superstitious people of the past and modern sophisticates hold to the belief that the predisposition to sickness lies in the fabric—whether clay or chromosome—of our being.

The Saltus River—for which Salcininki is named—is a dark narrow river that flows generally north-to-south through the city. The word *Saltus* means "cold", and I don't doubt that's true in this part of the world.

We heard from everyone that recent winters have been mild—this in a region known for fierce winters. Marija and Gintautas were aware of the possibility of global warming, but the Bielawskis were not. I tried to joke that, in the near future, Vilnius would be a seaport on the Baltic Sea, but Emilia changed the joke by replacing "decades" with "centuries" so as not to upset them.

Near the river is the distillery that Danislav told us about three years ago. The distillery was owned in the previous century by the local nobles, a family named "Wagner". At some point it was converted to a creamery and then back to a distillery. Gorbachev had it closed down in the 1980s as part of the crackdown on excessive alcohol consumption. I had expected to see ruins, but the building is in remarkably good repair, with two large silver tanks standing outside a warehouse.

The house where the Wagner family resided is across the street from the distillery. The building, which survived the World War in good repair, is an impressive two or three story mansion swaddled with trees. It currently houses a music academy.

There is a monument to the Wagner family behind the church. A plaque on the cairn announces in Latin an event involving "P—Michala Wagner." The top of the plaque bears the acronym "D.O.M." The year indicated is 1812, quite a significant year in history.

The church at Salcininki is a tall gray structure with two steeples. There are no statues and no windows in the walls. The Nazis burned the previous church, so the new one, built in Soviet times, blands right in with the nondescript architecture of the 1950s and 1960s.

The cemetery is to the side of the church. It is a spacious place and better organized than the cemetery in Turgeli, with the graves arranged in precisely defined rows rather than willy-nilly. It is also flatter. As in Turgeli, headstones come in an amazing variety of size, shape, and color. Demarcated by railings, family plots are larger than what we see in America. These plots often include two or three separate headstones of different ages and designs. As in Turgeli, spouses are frequently buried side-by-side. And plots are privately tended, which means they are in greatly different states of upkeep.

We visited two plots. Albinus Pupalaigis, Marija's husband, rests under a simple black headstone. (Albinus managed the fish farms in the vicinity before his sudden death in 1996. Previously, he managed the creamery aside the lost cemetery in Zaltuny.) Marija and Albinas will be together for eternity, since her name has already been etched in the stone. The other grave belonged to Paulina (Bielawski) Wasilewski and her husband Josef. Paulina was my grandfather's half-sister. My grandfather was still in Lithuania—it was Russia then—when she was born, so he would have known her as a child. Her dates are 1905-1988. Josef's are 1906-92. They have separate stones.

As we did with the Bielawski family, we took our leave of Marija and Gintautas at the gates of a cemetery.

The ride back to Vilnius was done in an expeditious manner. Kestas was flying along at a hectic pace and traffic was light. The traffic in the heart of Vilnius fades rapidly after rush hour and there is very little traffic in the countryside. The only "traffic jam" we encountered outside Vilnius was a herd of slow-moving cows. These were amazingly dense creatures, who ignored the impatient blare of the horn and didn't know what to do when the car approached. Their front legs turned one way, their hind legs turned the other way, and they kept walking in the middle of the road. We eventually got through with a minimum of delay and a maximum of dust and dirty bovine looks. If looks could kill, we'd be human rump roast.

After a brief rest at the hotel we strolled to Gedimino St. and settled for supper at Vidudienis restaurant, where we had dined the night before. Babci had pork chops with rice and I had vegetable soup. I think Babci had the better of the dishes.

We walked back to the hotel on Zygimantis *Gatve*, which runs on the south side of the Neris River. We viewed the strange amalgam of architecture we noticed during our first visit. Near the Green Bridge there is an immense, very distinguished, four-story palace constructed of walls of huge stones and a number of gated entrances. Adjacent to it is a cluster of one-story dilapidated wood structures that would not be out of place in Malakonys.

Mass was getting out of St. Raphael's when we crossed the Green Bridge and climbed the stairs to Snipiskiu St. This was 7:35 PM. The crowd consisted mostly of elderly ladies in snoods, sweaters, and swollen feet. An entrepreneur could make a fortune selling canes.

The Church of St. Raphael is an active parish dating from the eighteenth century. The exterior of the church is somewhat dingy, but it is distinguished by two graceful Baroque towers that rise high over the central nave. Tall in themselves, the towers appear taller because of the impressive location of the church. Situated on a hill at the northern end of the Green Bridge, the church is visible for quite a distance from the opposite side of the Neris. In this location the church has been featured in photographs and postcards for more than a century.

June 9

A third great day of family history!

Emilia arrived precisely at 10:00 AM accompanied by a new driver named Karl, a heavyset Polish man with bright blue eyes. He was more careful than Kestas and certainly drove more slowly. Perhaps he had warning that Lithuanian "smokies" were prowling the roads. We were, in fact, stopped twice, once for a roadside emission test (we passed), the second at a border checkpoint a few miles south of Salcininki. This checkpoint was somewhat unusual, since we were not technically at a border. In the middle of literally nowhere, there was a guard shack and a security arm over the road—this, despite the fact that the road lies in a flat and picturesque field maybe a quarter mile wide.

The flat land south of Salcininki contains islands of thick forests—they turned into continents as we proceeded. The tall trees look like pines, but there are plenty of firs and a thin white variety I took for birches or poplars. The combination of flat open land and closed forest produces a strange distortion when the road curves upward and the trees creep forward. It looked like we were driving into a green wall or box.

Our first stop was the apartment of Wladyslawa Kucsynska. This was in Dieveniskes, population eight hundred.

It's not clear what "Dieveniskes" means. Our hosts suggested that the word means a conjunction of nine roads. It could also have reference to a place of pagan sacrifice in the long ago. Whatever the correct translation, the village is old, being described in thirteenth century records. The chief twentieth century attractions appear to be the abundant hunting and fishing available.

Despite its age, Dieveniskes is an unremarkable town. It consists of small bungalows arranged near the streets and a few three-story Soviet-era housing complexes. The sidewalks are very narrow, the streets are tiny and scattered, and the complexes look to be located at the perimeter of town. The greatest activity we saw was an outdoor flea market held in what appeared to be the town center. This consisted of a few stores, a rock monument we didn't stop to examine, and a concentration of people, two of whom were, as I've described, seated on the curb where they unceremoniously passed the bottle to Emilia's vexation.

The housing situation in Dieveniskes is the same as in Salcininki. The complexes are not maintained from the outside, but the apartments are attractive. Wladyslawa's was, anyway—or the room we ate in was. This was the dining area or living room. On one side of the large table was a glass-enclosed china cabinet. On the other side a black-and-gold drape hung from the wall.

As in Marija's apartment, I didn't see any personal photographs on the walls. And the furniture was close to floor level—this may have had something to do with the fact that I'm somewhat longer than the village people.

The dinner Wladyslawa prepared was fit for travelers from a far-off land. It was the largest spread we encountered in Lithuania, which is saying something. There were several meats, two kinds of fish, a number of salads, including a delicious potato salad and coleslaw, which they called *kapusta*. In Polish Jersey City *kapusta* means "cabbage", as in ham-and-cabbage, but in Polish Dieveniskes *kapusta* means what we call "coleslaw". They were familiar with *Kapusta* used as a surname, as in the gentleman buried near my grandfather in Holy Cross Cemetery, but didn't think it as funny as I did.

The highlights of the meal were peeled hard-boiled eggs dressed in tomato berets. A battalion of these tiny soldiers arranged on a field of lettuce was delightful to look at and almost too esthetic to eat.

Wladyslawa's son, Tomas, is in his early twenties. He's a soldier stationed in Vilnius. Tomas is tall and tan, with a crew cut that makes him resemble the actor Ricky Schroeder.

We were joined by Wladyslawa's brother, Josef Masian, and his wife. Josef is a heavyset man in his fifties with a Vandyke beard, glasses, and a receding hairline. He's a gregarious personality who liked his food and his drink. He insisted on keeping every glass filled, starting with his own. The main beverage was a Lithuanian liquor we first drank in Michail Bielawski's house. We were warned then and we heard the same warning in Dieveniskes, not that anyone paid attention to it in either place—a few drinks will make you mellow, but too many drinks will cause your head to pound.

I had to beg off refills on more than one occasion with the excuses that "I'm not a drinking man" and "I need to stay awake." None of these worked with Josef, who really enjoyed himself.

Both Josef and his wife are teachers. As with Michail Bielawski's sons, both have experienced difficulties getting paid. There was a time in the recent past when they weren't paid for more than six months. Tomas is paid only 1,100 *litas* a month, which is less than $400. And he's a soldier, which is a class you'd think the government would want to keep happy.

Josef was surprisingly blunt in criticizing the government. He made fun of the Soviet leadership, picking on Brezhnev, who he mocked as being more interested in collecting medals than in governing. He also belittled the current regime in Vilnius. His attitude has to do with the difficulties in getting paid. It also has to do with the issue of safety. He claimed the area was generally safe, but that "gypsies" had been allowed to live nearby, causing some concern. He said they had to lock their doors because of the gypsies.

Josef also complained about Belarus and about the border situation. To cross, they need an identification card, which is good on either a daily or a monthly basis. These people spend a lot of time going back and forth into the forest and getting cards on a temporary basis is a nuisance. A greater nuisance is getting caught without a card. There are guard towers, patrols, and listening devices, where before there were risk-free passages through the woods.

Josef admitted that considerable contraband crossed between borders. Prices for liquor, to name one necessary commodity, are low in Lithuania.

But the prices are lower in Belarus, which tempts people to sneak Bacchos into Lithuania.

We were joined midway into dinner by Anna, Danislav's sister. Anna is a tiny lady around seventy years of age. She has a round face and prominent nose. Except for the nose, Anna bore a startling resemblance to my Aunt Blanche.

Anna was quite emotional. She cried when she met us. She also joined, rather angrily, in the conversation about the border problems. She has difficulty combing the woods for berries and mushrooms and this annoys her greatly.

We stayed with Wladyslawa for about three hours, much longer than we planned. After considerable toasts, hugs, and pictures, we took our leave of this fine, friendly, family.

With Anna as our guide, we drove to Girdziunai, which is only a few miles away. The awful road we took three years ago is now inside Belarus and inaccessible. So, we had to take an even more awful road a little to the north. The road was nothing more than a track cut in the deep woods. It's unpaved, of course, and wildly uneven.

There was a small village in a clearing about midway on the trip. At this point, the land rises steeply to the south. The village—Anna called it "Gudenia" (phonetic)—consisted of five or six houses placed together in the woods on the flat northern side.

On the return trip we squeezed past a tractor parked on the incline beside the road. A few workers were lounging nearby. I joked that the reason the Lithuanian economy wasn't booming was that too many workers took too many breaks. Emilia liked that observation.

The road finally emerged from the woods and joined the larger road just in front of Girdziunai. I immediately remembered the place. The Storta house is the first or second as one enters Girdziunai from the west. Little has changed since our last visit. The house is still bright yellow. Immediately behind it is an enclosed garden. Two large barns stand behind the house to the right. One of them is a woodshed crammed to capacity with logs. An outhouse is behind the barns.

The house is on the ancestral Storta property, which can be traced in church documents to 1801. On this trip we have had the privilege of visiting the places where both my Polish grandparents were born.

Josef Masian told us that Girdziunai is pronounced "Yush-zoon-ney" rather than as "Gird-zoon-ney", as it looks on paper to an American. He claimed the word means "the forest listens".

The Storta family met us at the entrance of their home. Danislav has gained considerable weight and uses a cane to get around. His face is deeply tanned and much more jowly than I remember. His thick hair is white. He is seventy two years of age.

Danislav has some disease of the legs that requires an operation. It's difficult to say what the disease is—perhaps it involves the heart or the circulation. I gave a donation toward the operation, which will cost several thousand *litas*.

Of all the relatives we met in Lithuania, Danislav was the most interested in money—in getting it and in talking about it. This led to some uncomfortable questions about pensions, salaries, and health care costs.

Danislav's wife was present, as was Josef, his son, and Teresa, his daughter. Josef's wife is an especially charming lady. Their two-year-old-son woke up during our visit. He shows promise of being in the heavyweight division, since he sat on the table and tasted adult food, including the kielbasa.

Janina, Danislav's third child—she's the doctor in Salcininki—could not be present. But her husband and children were. He's a pleasant black-haired, mustachioed fellow who looked more "white collar" than "blue collar".

We had the pleasure of meeting Adela, Danislav's second sister. Compared to Anna, she's tall, thin, and angular. She and Anna became quite agitated at times—maybe they don't hit it off—which frustrated Emilia, who couldn't keep up with all the conversations going on.

For the second time we heard about the border troubles with Belarus and about the unresponsiveness of the government in Vilnius. I teased about the possibility of forming an independent Republic of Girdziunai—I was informed that people had been arrested for suggesting something similar during the time of independence in 1991. This area of Lithuania is heavily Polish and Russian. The people here didn't prosper during communism, but they weren't as inconvenienced as the Baltic people to the north and west. They're not prospering under capitalism and they're worried that they'll be abused by the new Lithuanian regime, which they see as unsympathetic toward Slavs. And their experience with the Republic of Belarus, an artificially created country with no historical foundation, has not been friendly. They see themselves as trapped and friendless, and they may not be wrong in their assessment.

We didn't learn anything new genealogically—there's a point of diminishing returns in traveling to the "old country". I was, however, able to fulfill a dream that emerged three years ago on the occasion of our first visit. I walked from one end of Girdziunai to the other.

The unpaved road that runs through Girdziunai is uneven, marked in places by large rocks and by potholes filled with water from the recent rain. The mixture of dirt, mud, and water produced a strong earthy odor. Decidedly not an urban smell. The road meanders in direction roughly from west to east. It makes a few soft turns, so that you can't see the entire road from any one point, but none of the turns is particularly sharp. The southern (Belarus) portion of Girdziunai is hilly, rising steeply from the road. This portion is generally clear of trees. If any farming goes on, it must be in this area.

There are a few houses on the southern side of the road, but the majority of houses are located on the northern (Lithuanian) side, which is far more woodsy. I counted about thirty houses. Danislav says a third are unoccupied. There are a number of unpainted houses, which must be the vacant ones. The occupied houses are painted yellow, with a few blues ones mixed in for diversity. The houses all look the same age and style—there are a lot of windows, all rather large and low to the floor. Each property is self-contained, with tiny wood fences separating one from the other. A few are set back off the road; some, like the Storta house, lie directly on the road.

It takes about twenty minutes to walk from one end of Girdziunai to the other. The road ends unceremoniously a few yards in front of the last house, a rather large one. (This is the side of the village our Juchniewicz ancestors lived in.) If the road continues past this house, it merges seamlessly with the forest.

It's possible at this point to enter the woods on the northern side. A short walk leads to the Gauja River, which runs behind the houses. The river is not visible from the Storta house or from any point on the road. It's impossible to judge distance on this portion of the hike, but my guess is that the river is probably less than thirty or forty yards to the north of the row of houses.

The clearing we approached was quite scenic and about as open as open can get in these woods. This area may serve as a communal place for the village—it looked perfect for a picnic. The Gauja, which can be traced on maps as far away as Dieveniskes, is narrow at this point, running quietly beyond a slope thick with grass and foliage. Two horses stood tied in the clearing. One was agitated, shying and neighing vigorously. On our approach, the horse calmed down and stood attentively.

It was wonderful to fulfill the dream of touring the ancestral village of Girdziunai. I now know what is at the end of the road. It was also a strange experience. Girdziunai is a poor place, something out of the nineteenth century. It was easy to imagine my grandparents and *their grandparents* making the same trek from their homes to the clearing at the river. There's a real sense of a village frozen in time. Yet there are telephone poles near the road and cars parked in the dirt lanes. And there are political pressures and social uncertainties for the citizens of this obscure place.

The strangeness lies in the awareness of straddling two centuries simultaneously—family history is an extension of my own experience. Our records here date to 1801—Laurynas and Elzbieta Storta were born in the eighteenth century. The feeling of the past is very strong and the presence of the past is very apparent. Yet the year 2001 is half a year away. The future is also a palpable presence on a hike that encompassed two centuries in a half hour.

The day was running late, so we took our leave of Danislav and his family and, wishing them good health, returned to Vilnius. There wasn't much conversation on the drive back, since everyone was talked out and exhausted. At the hotel we said farewell to Karl and to Emilia, who had been our able voice for three days.

I had walked where family had walked two hundred years ago. When we arrived in Vilnius, I took another walk, this one completely situated in the twenty-first century. I traipsed into town and bought McDonald's for a late snack—a Big Mac and fries for Babci and a fish sandwich and fries for me. There was something deeply satisfying eating fast food and sipping coffee out of a Styrofoam container. It was a feeling of being home in my own time.

June 10

After three days we had run out of relatives to visit. It was time to tour the Old Town!

Our walk began at 11:30. We crossed the Green Bridge, took pictures at the Opera House, and strolled past the Cathedral of St. Stanislaw to Pilies *Gatve*, the main street in the Old Town. It was Saturday, so that helped, but Pilies St. was more lively than during our first visit. The buildings were in much better repair and they were far more colorful, being painted bright yellow and pink and blue. There were more restaurants than previously, especially near the Cathedral and around the former Town Hall, which is about halfway to the Dawn Gate at the other end of the road. There was an outdoor café located in a space directly in front of the Town Hall; this space had been a parking lot three years ago. The Medininki Cellar, an open-air restaurant near the Russian Orthodox Church of the Holy Spirit, was still in existence and the food was as good as I remembered from our previous visit. Babci had chicken pancakes and I had a delicious cabbage and mushroom appetizer followed by potatoes mixed with cheese.

Pilies St. reminds me of Greenwich Village in New York City. Artists display their works along the walls of the buildings and there's a well-organized display of art in the courtyard near St. Nicholas Church. The artists sit on folding chairs and watch the customers. When they note some interest in a particular work they stand and start to hawk their creations in a medley of languages—a little English, a little Russian, a little Lithuanian, and a lot of oil and watercolor. Some of the paintings are beautiful—the favorite themes were the Cathedral, the Church of St. Anne's, and nature scenes—but most are too large to carry on board the plane. We purchased a small, nicely colored, painting of St. Anne's from an artist near St. John's *Gatve*.

The same flea market we visited three years ago still exists on Pilies St. Every stand sells identical items—jewelry, artwork, toys, kitchen utensils, and assorted categories of trinkets. Religious themes are prominent, especially the Pensive Christ, that rather sad icon in which the Savior sits with his hand slapped against his forehead, as if he were trying not to notice the sins of the world. Of course, amber items are featured at every stand. Amber can be purchased as jewelry and individually in all shapes, sizes, and colors. Yellowish specimens predominate, but there were highly attractive pieces in a popsicle combination of cream and yellow. The salespeople insist that their amber contains fossilized insects and they allow you to inspect the pieces using magnifying lenses. I'm certain that the amber I bought has an insect inside—I can clearly see the wings and legs of what looks to be a mosquito.

Legend has it that amber originated in the tears of the sea goddess, Jurate, who cried when Perkunas, the thunder god, destroyed her castle after catching her in a compromising position with a mortal. The scientific explanation for the origin of amber is no less amazing. Some forty million years ago—not the age of dinosaurs, but close enough—global warming caused an increase in the secretion of resin in the vast pine forests that grew along the coasts and on a landmass swallowed long ago by what became the Baltic Sea. Before the sea swallowed the forests, the resin accumulated on the ground, capturing everything in its path. What's submerged eventually rises—the sea keeps sins, but lets amber escape. Through the centuries, amber fragments surfaced in vast quantities on the Baltic coast, producing a trade in jewelry and artwork that preceded recorded history.

I can picture this happening. A mosquito takes a break on the bark of a tree. A droplet of sap falls on it, immobilizing it forever. Forty million years later I'm standing on Pilies St. in the Old Town in Vilnius looking at the same mosquito through a magnifying glass. We both look astonished.

It's sad to report that the *rutos knygos* where I saw the Barnes & Noble shopping bag three years ago is out-of-business. But there are a number of bookstores in the area, including three large ones on Gedimino St. These cater to the nearby university.

One of the more interesting shops was in an alley across from the flea market. (This was the same alley where the sad-sack Brezhnev clone sold his medals.) This very cramped shop specialized in antique icons and old books. Really old books. I dared not examine them, since they were in Lithuanian and in Russian and many were falling apart. We called these kinds of books "M&M books" in the Sale Annex days—the boards melt in your hands. There didn't seem to be any order to the arrangement of the articles and the books were badly stacked. Inspecting one, you tempted gravity. Some of the books looked too fragile to survive the fall.

The shop catered to God and to Caesar—Tsar, I should write—by offering political posters and portraits for sale. A huge poster of N. Lenin was near the entrance. Further inside, two posters of A. Hitler leaned amid the clutter. *Der Fuhrer* was in his Teutonic Knights pose—a theme that would be a hit among the proud descendants of Vytautas, who defeated the Teutonic Order in the Battle of Tannenburg in 1410. This battle not being widely known among customs agents on either side of the Atlantic, the poster would have required lengthy explanation.

We didn't visit as many churches this year—the guidebook lists thirty four—since we took it easy and spent a lot of time shopping. We did, however, manage to visit some of the more prominent ones.

The Jesuit Church of St. Casimir, adjacent to the Town Hall, is the oldest surviving Baroque church in Vilnius. The exterior is famous and is often portrayed in pictures, postcards, and artwork. The church is pink in color and has that "I am a façade" look of many churches in Lithuania, being tall and ponderous. There are no statues on the outside walls. A cupola at the top of the church supports a black crown and gold cross. The cupola, which is forty meters high, was built in the late eighteenth century. Surprisingly, the crown and cross were added during the Nazi occupation.

The interior of the church is tall and airy. The center nave is defined by beautiful pinkish-salmon columns. The portraits of Casimir and of J. Christ that hang above the altar are not impressive. The portraits are colorful, but overdone and incompatible with the somber columns.

The first church on the site of St. Casimir's was built in the early seventeenth century, but it has not had a lucky history. The Jesuits, who founded the church and who run it now, were barred from Vilnius from 1773–1919. They were ejected again during the Soviet occupation. The church has been devastated by fire three times in its history. The French army used the church as a granary in 1812. In Soviet times the church was rechristened as the wonderfully-named *Museum of Atheism*.

St. Casimir is the patron saint of Lithuania. He is also the patron saint of bachelors. He was born in Vilnius is 1458 and died in 1484. Casimir was the son of Casimir III, King of Poland, and of Elizabeth of Austria. He became king of Hungary at the age of fifteen, but his tenure was not successful. He resigned the kingship and returned to Poland, where he forsook politics and pursued the religious life. He's buried in the Cathedral.

The Town Hall is a bright building, spanking white in color and with six hefty columns. A town hall has stood on this site since the early sixteenth century. The present building dates from the late 1700s. It resembles the Cathedral in its classical design and portentous size—this resemblance is due to the fact that both buildings had the same architect, Laurynas Gucevicius. A long row of flagpoles stretches in a garden that runs contiguous with the new café that replaced the parking lot. The flags represent the nations Lithuania has diplomatic relations with, currently more than fifty countries. There are a number of restaurants, beer halls, and bakeries flanking the Town Hall. The Church of St. Casimir is to the left. A large hotel in a modern glass frame—the building is not new; dark glass covers the original brickwork—is immediately behind the Town Hall. A busy taxi stand is in front of the hotel.

The area around the Town Hall is upscale and happening—it's *now* in the midst of oldness—but this place has witnessed the dark side of history. The space in front of the Town Hall—where the flags and café are—long served as the public gallows. There was no shortage of victims. The place must have been jumping—the trapdoors, anyway—in 1863, when hundreds were brought to Vilnius and hanged for their involvement with the failed rebellion against Tsar Alexander II.

The famous Basilian Gate is a short walk from the Town Hall. This gate—an archway, really; there is no gate—dates from the late eighteenth century. Built in the Baroque style, the Gate has no right angles and consists entirely of wavy lines and sinewy contours. The Gate can serve as a symbol of the rebirth and ripening of Vilnius. In 1997 the Gate was drab and unpainted. It looked centuries old. In 2000 it's revived in beautiful creams, yellows, and pinks. It looks ready to stand for another two centuries.

Which is more than can be said for the Church of the Basilian Monastery. There's been some work on the exterior—the broken stairs have been paved and the walls painted a dull yellow—but little else has changed since 1997. Probably, little changed for a long time before 1997. Although services are held, the church remains in disrepair, with chipped walls and interior scaffolding. You get the feeling that the scaffolding is holding the roof up, so there's no inclination to explore. Not that there's much to explore, since it's impossible to enter more than fifty feet inside.

The church stands on the left side of a courtyard that curves round to a cul-de-sac. Adam Mickiewicz lived for a time in an apartment at the end of the courtyard. A squarish bell tower is to the right near the Gate. It's an impressive chunk of a building about three stories high and with few windows. A printing press existed on the grounds in the eighteenth century, one of only two presses in Vilnius at the time. Three Orthodox saints named John, Anthony, and Eustace, were martyred on the grounds in the fourteenth century. The area behind the Gate looks old—easily, the oldest-looking section of Vilnius we saw. There's an atmosphere of real decrepitude. There's also a sense of going backwards in time. Twenty steps off the vibrant happening comedy of Pilies *Gatve,* you're reflecting on the tragedies of long-dead poets and martyrs.

We next visited the Church of the Holy Spirit, the major Russian Orthodox church in Vilnius. The church is located near the Dawn Gate. It's set back from the street and on a slight incline. The area is park-like and peaceful. There's a monastery behind the church, which adds to the tranquility. I almost felt I should be walking on tiptoe with my index finger pressed to my lips.

The church was built in the Baroque style in the early seventeenth century. The dome and the wildly imaginative icons were added in the nineteenth century. The altar is bright green and black and the walls and columns are covered with a vast number of portraits of saints and patriarchs. Included on the walls are glass-enclosed vestments, presumably worn by the worthies portrayed. Relics of the three martyrs killed in the courtyard beyond the Basilian Gate are interred beneath the altar.

We tried to take a side trip to the Jewish ghetto established in World War Two. This is accessible along Rudninkiu *Gatve,* which commences near the Town Hall. Unfortunately, we didn't get more than a block or two in. The area is depressed and slummy, with lots of young men milling about. The streets are narrow, the houses continuous rows of run-down three-story tenements—there are no bright yellows and pinks and blues in this section. It didn't look like an area tourists should visit, not when we were carrying all our money in our pouches.

The streets look like something out of a 1930s photograph—crowded, dark, depressed, and black-and-white. The only missing elements are the Jews.

The last active synagogue in Vilnius is near Rudninkiu *Gatve.* It is a low, dark white building partially concealed behind shrubbery and locked gates. The building is not much used given "the events of the twentieth century," which is how we heard the World War and the Holocaust referred to. The history of the Nazi occupation of Vilnius is terrible to consider. The ghetto lasted from July, 1941, to September, 1943. The major killing field was in the forest near the village of Ponary, seven miles to the south of Vilnius. Between the roving madness of the *Einsatzgruppen* and the organized destruction that systematically led from Rudninkiu *Gatve* to the quarries in Ponary, more than 140,000 Jews were killed.

The destruction of the Jews of Lithuania is particularly tragic, given their historical reception and role in society. Jews have lived in Lithuania, mostly in

Vilnius, since the fifteenth century. Until the events of the twentieth century, Jews served as merchants and scholars and were left undisturbed to study the Talmud. Vilnius was called the "Jerusalem of Lithuania" because of the extensive Jewish community and rabbinical schools located here. Everything is gone now, except for a single synagogue and for the approximately five thousand Jews who remain.

The cosmopolitan nature of Vilnius and the short distances involved guarantee that knowledge of the "events of the twentieth century" could not have remained a secret as they occurred.

Church burnings and confiscations, hundreds of freedom fighters hanged, three martyrs slain for their faith, 140,000 Jews slain for no rational purpose—the mind grows numb in the vastness of the tragedies thrown up on the shores of history. We had walked for almost five hours—and we had traveled a long way from the Pilies St. flea market to consideration of the charnel of Ponary. And we hadn't visited the former KGB headquarters on Gedimino St., where even more recent atrocities are documented.

The purpose of our trip to the Amber Country was family history. It's horrifying to consider all the families slain in the mischief of history, and all the families affected by the killings, and all the families who raised individuals who perpetrated atrocities, and all the families who raised individuals who stood idly by while monsters were at work. It's impossible to comprehend the enormity of these events. Psychology is no help, other than the bandying of diagnoses. Religion is no help, other than the cataloging of sins. Literature is no help—if these events were not part of the historical record, they would not be believed in works of fiction.

It was horrifying to think that these terrible events, although widely dispersed in time, occurred within a short geographical distance—no more than a few miles—of each other. And it's especially horrifying to think that the Holocaust is part of the living memory of literally thousands of families. There's no "ancient history" on Rudninkiu *Gatve*. These thoughts were almost enough to make me run back to the Hotel Naujasis Vilnius and hide—but my feet hurt too badly to proceed at anything other than a slow walk.

June 11

Another day of walking the Old Town—and walking and *walking* the Old Town. Along the way, we revisited some old friends among churches and made a new friend.

We managed a brief visit to St. John's Church near Vilnius University. We weren't able to visit three years ago and we still couldn't locate the main entrance, which is somewhere in the courtyard of the university, but we slipped in a side door after services and took a quick look around before the sexton closed the lights and chased everyone out.

St. John's dates to the fourteenth century, nearly coterminous with the founding of Vilnius. The present building dates from 1737. Like St. Casimir's, it did not fare well in the twentieth century. It suffered in former times because of its association with the university and whatever subversive influences existed in academia. In Soviet times it became the *Museum of Science* and was badly gutted.

The interior of the church is huge, with a high altar and two side altars. The center nave contains two aisles of nondescript pews. A large chandelier hangs over the pews. There is considerable statuary along the walls honoring long dead clerics and academics. The spacious back end of the church held an exhibition of university publications and artwork.

Several open confessionals stand along the walls. The thought occurred that sins would be a matter of social shame as much as of moral conscience. One's voice might be audible, and one's face would be visible. And so would the priest's! I don't know which would be more revealing.

After an hour of shopping—it's hard to make decisions when all the trinkets are the same—we took a break for beer, soup, and salad, at a German restaurant named Dravo. The restaurant was located in a picturesque enclave aside the Vilnius River.

We then walked to the St. Anne's and Bernardines complex, architecturally the most beautiful part of Vilnius. The complex is visible in its entirety from this approach, which makes for a grand view and for some fine photographs. As we approach the complex we cross a small bridge that spans the Vilnius River. This is more impressive sounding than it is in reality, since the bridge is only a few feet wide. The river is narrow at this point and deeply set. There's a statue of the ubiquitous Adam Mickiewicz on a small lawn to the south of the churches. The spires of St. Michael's are visible to the west—St. Michael's is a closed church currently serving as a museum. Across the street is a one-story, clay-colored building that was once a convent. St. Anne's stands at the curb—the sidewalk is only a few paces wide. The Church of the Bernardines looms behind it, parallel to the river. A large park is behind the complex. A bell tower stands to the side of St. Anne's. The tower matches the church in style and brickwork, but is much more modern, having been built in the nineteenth century.

The interior of St. Anne's has changed many times across the years, but the exterior is pretty much unchanged from its foundation. The church was built of a number of varieties of red and brown bricks. The entrance consists of a central arch and two side arches, all rather low and narrow. There are two steeples. A series of windows, tall and very narrow, run along the side naves. Several buttresses stand to the sides of the church, but these are purely decorative.

The face of the church is wonderfully decorative, with a number of turrets and rills looping over the arches. The stained glass is cleverly inserted between the rills. The glass rises straight and stiff, whereas the brickwork bends and twists and snakes and frolics as it flows along the wall. It's almost an inversion of nature, quite as if the rocks in a pond started to swim in water that grew rigid.

The Church of the Bernardines is a huge, heavy building erected, like St. Anne's, in the sixteenth century. It is very tall and superbly rectangular. The church is built of lighter brick than St. Anne's, being more pinkish than brownish red, especially near the roof. There is a large mural of the Risen Christ above the central nave. The picture is not particularly attractive and cheapens the colossal effect.

The outside of the church has been renovated—the scaffolds from three years ago are gone—but there has been only modest improvement in the interior. The walls are not painted and the floor is not finished. The altar and the pulpit, both of which are wood, look new, but the altar is, in fact, very old, dating to the late 1700s. Electric lights have been strung over the pews like stringers over a pier. It must be impressive to see the interior aglow on a snowy winter's evening. Someday, we'll have to visit in winter.

To the left of the portal is a large, but dim, mural. This painting depicts a walled city that must represent Vilnius at an early period. But it was hard to make out details, since only the lower left was clear. The rest of the painting was either unrestored or irreparably damaged.

A large painting of the crucified Christ hangs high over the altar, but it, too, is ghostly, the image being nearly invisible from our vantage.

I ask myself why, in this city of beautiful churches, St. Anne's and the Church of the Bernardines are so distinctive and so moving. There are a number of answers. Their effect may have to do with the involvement of these buildings in the tragedies of history. Napoleon visited St. Anne's on his way to Moscow in 1812 and the Church of the Bernardines was closed for its subversive influence in the bloody revolt of 1863. Their effect may also have to do with the solid simplicity of the Church of the Bernardines and, by way of visual contrast, with the architectural virtuosity of St. Anne's. The intricacy of the walls becomes a kind of projective test in brick. The front of St. Anne's is a face with a mouth bent in mourning. But wait. It's not a face, but the mask of someone pretending to be sad. No, it's not a mask, but something inanimate, perhaps a chalice or a bell or a sacred artifact. No, it's not inanimate, but something sentient, although not human, maybe the guardian of the city or the guardian of the portal between this realm and the place where sins are counted. But it's not supernatural, it's—it's—you get the idea. Who would have thought that Gothic architecture could be so fascinating?

The effect may have to do with the arrangement of churches. St. Anne's is a little girl, the Church of the Bernardines is her older brother. They're waiting at the curb to cross the street—and they need to look both ways, given how they drive in this place.

St. Anne's was closed, but we were able to enter the nearby bell tower for a small fee. A fairly steep staircase leads to an altar about one or two flights up. The descent is made by way of a separate, and less decorative, staircase separated from the first by a wall. There's not much to see on the second level. The altar is bare, except for a long white cloth. Candles lie everywhere, including in niches in the walls and on the floor, where they rest in tiny cups. The tower rises an additional one or two stories above the altar.

A young man met us at the entrance. He escorted us a third of the way up and indicated that we should complete the ascent on our knees. At this suggestion I told him we are Americans and that we don't get on our knees for anyone. That didn't wash, so I said Babci has arthritis in her legs, which is true, and can't get on her knees, which isn't true, but he didn't know that. There was no excuse in my case—but my feet *were* sore and I was limping from a callus that felt like a nail.

We walked along the Vilnius River into Kalnu Park. This is the large park that begins at the Church of the Bernardines and curves round to the Cathedral. The park was clean, although the grass was high and uncut. It looked safe and family oriented, with a small amusement park and playground, as well as tennis courts. There were a number of young men and women openly drinking beer. There was no rowdiness, or none that we observed.

There's a modern statue of Gediminas, the founder of historical Vilnius, at the entrance of the park near the Cathedral. Gediminas, who hailed from Trakai, had a dream near here that a huge iron wolf was howling. He was inspired by the dream to found the city and the castle on the hill. Of course, the area was inhabited long before Gediminas entered REM sleep. Human habitations have been uncovered dating back to 1000 BCE. Individual tribes were identified by traders in the years of the Roman Republic. Feudalism had taken hold by the tenth century. Feudalism lasted, in one guise or another, until the twentieth century, after which another *-ism* stupefied the ordinary folk.

Gediminas stands on a tall column, so far from the sidewalk the particulars of the sculpture are invisible to anyone with corrected vision. He affects a proud pose, a nationalistic pose, but he carries neither sword nor dagger. And he is looking in the *wrong* direction. He faces Kalnu Park rather than the city proper and is standing at a right angle to the Old Town. He has his back turned on the heart of Vilnius. Maybe he dislikes imports from China.

We visited the Cathedral for the last time—we always come back to the Cathedral, as to an old friend. Our destination was the chapel of St. Casimir, which was closed, unfortunately. We were able to stand at the gate and peek inside.

The chapel, which is in the Baroque style, is a small room. Probably, it can't hold more than fifty people—twenty five, if kneeling. But the chapel is the same height as the Cathedral, which is disorienting. It's like staring inside a stovetop hat, a comparison which is entirely appropriate, since the walls are black as they ascend to the ceiling. This being the Baroque style, the walls are generously ornamented with bas-reliefs of angels, saints, and local heroes.

The altar is heavily decorated. A large bas-relief depicts St. Casimir entering heaven. He's received into bliss by the Blessed Mother, who has a broad smile on her face. It's quite a rarity to see Mary smiling.

Above the tabernacle is a small 1520 painting of a *three-handed* St. Casimir. No one knows why the artist painted a third hand. One conjecture is that the artist wanted to depict the miraculous power of the saint. Another conjecture is that the artist wanted to signify the number of Casimir's accomplishments in the three realms of spirit, mind, and matter. A third conjecture is that the artist was supernaturally inspired to paint three hands. A final conjecture is that the artist simply lost count.

A gold goblet-shaped pulpit is to the left of the altar. The pulpit rests on a silver eagle, symbolizing St. John the Evangelist. The gaudiness of the pulpit appears excessive. It resembles a car in a Wildwood amusement ride—a car in the Whip, maybe, or a serpent on the carousel—more than it does a place of religious instruction.

Four statues, representing early kings of Lithuania, surround the altar on pedestals inserted into the walls. Their silver frames blend seamlessly into the décor. Unlike Gediminas, these grim figures hold swords and spears that extend over the pews in menacing gestures.

Since this was our last day in Vilnius, we wanted to dine at *Stiklai Alade*, one of the better restaurants in town. This took some hunting, however, and we were dragging by the hour, which was closing on six. The restaurant was located on Ganno *Gatve* near Vilnius University, but the street was difficult to locate.

I let Babci wait by the flea market on Pilies and hiked a few blocks to locate the restaurant. This was my chance to give her the slip, but I passed up the chance. I couldn't let Babci find her way to the hotel by her lonesome. She would have to find the nearest gendarme and inquire, "*Ger jest Hotelu Naujasis Vilnius?*" I don't think the answer would be much help.

I couldn't leave Babci behind, not after she had walked so long and had been so good a trooper.

The *Stiklai Alade* restaurant is very tiny, with only a few tables. There is an underground dining room that is highly recommended. A wedding party was in progress, so the area was roped off. The décor of the downstairs dining area is supposed to be excellent, but the room we ate in wasn't bad. Babci faced the door. I faced the rear window, through which I had the satisfaction of seeing customer-after-customer turned away from a bakery that had just closed for the day. After so many years in retail nothing gives me greater pleasure than seeing the sales help wave customers off, "Sorry, we're closed for the night. Come back tomorrow." I have no idea how they say that in Lithuanian, but it must sound as sweet.

Babci had fish and vegetables. I had mushroom and barley soup followed by potatoes and vegetables. The former was adequate, tasting like what we call in the States "Scotch broth", but the latter was superb.

After dinner we hobbled back to the hotel, having completed our second journey to the Amber Country. The walk was slow and agonizing—we had been on our feet for five hours. We passed the last of the booths in the flea market on Pilies St. From there, we walked sadly upward to the Cathedral and to Gedimino *Gatve*. Leaving the Old Town, we passed McDonald's and the black glass of the Opera House and crossed the Green Bridge to Snipiskiu *Gatve*. When we reached the opposite shore of the Neris River, we turned and saluted our bronze friends on the bridge. Their arms were raised in frozen waves. Who knows whether we shall see them another time?

As we passed St. Raphael's we said good-by to our friends in Kalniskes and Salcininki and Dieveniskes and Girdziunai in the forest that listens. We can't say what the future will bring for them or for us, but we hope that kind deeds and good times merit a comparable return. Vilnius has awakened from the slumber of the centuries and the mosquito in my amber has left the Baltic region for a display case in New Jersey. That's a longer journey, made across millions of years, than any we can take.

June 12

Karl picked us up promptly at 10:00 AM. We proceeded without delay through the hectic traffic to Vilnius Airport. The airport was crowded but ran efficiently.

Our connection was in Copenhagen and a layover of five hours. This time, which seems excessive, was spent productively shopping for duty-free goods—cognac, mostly—and for lunch. There was a gigantic selection of goods for sale, but a limited selection of lunches. To a vegan like myself, the restaurants offered a bizarre selection of menus—spaghetti with fish, spaghetti with prawn, spaghetti with various kinds of meat. I couldn't find a bowl of spaghetti with tomato sauce simple and pure. I think I settled for a smorgasbord of side dishes that added up to a square meal.

Kathy and Kimberly Pecoraro met us at the airport and drove us to Emerson, where we picked up the car. The trip to Emerson was quite lively, with lots of questions and answers about what we saw and who we met. But there was an element of sadness, too, since this was the first trip overseas when Dad didn't greet us at the airport.

We didn't get lost on the way home, as would have happened if Dad drove. We didn't get stuck in traffic or lose the parking pass. We didn't quibble over directions. We didn't hear complaints about problems finding the correct terminal. We had visited places of great age and significance—the ancestral farms, the Old Town, various churches standing firm despite history's wobble, other churches standing firm only with the help of scaffolding. I carried an amber-encapsulated insect that died millions of years ago. Dad's seventy two years, a blink in the epochal procession, was more pertinent and more meaningful than all the events in this flow of time.

Dad's absence teaches that this immense stretch of time is, from the perspective of our individual lives, an illusion. Our short lives pass so quickly within the vast resin drip of time. We have so few moments, each of them precious. We try to catch them, but they're gone even as we reach to keep them from flowing into oblivion.

We have so few moments, but we have memories of the times Dad met us at the airport and we have each other, and that cushions the sadness that we go only so far—not very far, at that—in this huge and bewildering place.

Snipiskiu Gatve

For the record I would like to describe the layout of Snipiskiu *Gatve*. This was the street that led from the Hotel Naujasis Vilnius to the Green Bridge. We must have walked it twenty times in the ten days we stayed in Vilnius in 1997 and in 2000. I have a lot of fond memories of this *gatve*, memories the fonder for the realization that it's unlikely I will ever walk it again.

The hotel is located on the left side of Snipiskiu *Gatve*. There is a parking lot immediately in front of the entrance. No vehicles are allowed beyond this point. To the immediate right of the hotel is a supermarket and liquor store. Across from the supermarket is the Valstybine Universaline Parduotuve, a shell of a building that holds a number of concession stands selling clothing, perfumes, and trinkets. The milieu of the store was bargain basement, but the prices were in the penthouse. The Hotel Lietuva, which serves as a kind of cul-de-sac to Snipiskiu *Gatve*, is a short walk to the right from the supermarket.

To proceed to the Green Bridge we turned left at the supermarket. There is a furniture store to the immediate left. Above the store is a Greek restaurant. (This building is immediately behind the parking lot to the hotel.) There are a number of kiosks selling papers, cigarettes, and trolley tickets across from the furniture store. A stretch of untended grass separates the kiosks from the Valstybine.

A small passage separates the furniture store from another building—we call this arrangement "blocks" in America, although they are much smaller in scale on Snipiskiu. This section held two stores, one of which advertised Kodak products. The Planetarium was to the immediate right. The Planetarium is a small place. Maybe viewers get to see the sky above Lithuania and not the total night sky.

The next block holds four three-story apartment buildings followed by a tall two-story building that sits at a cuneal angle at the intersection of Snipiskiu and Kalvariju *Gatve*. The buildings appear to be very old but upscale, as many of the apartments have balconies. There is a large kiosk in front of the two-story building. This spot is a major trolley stop. It was jammed with pedestrians during the workdays.

There are no separations into blocks on the right side of Snipiskiu Gatve. Instead, there is a single long and old building. The portion closer to the hotel was a two-story building that held a restaurant on ground level. The portion of the building closer to the street became St. Raphael's Church. I know the building is old—I have seen photographs of the building taken around 1900 in a book entitled *Vilnius in Old Postcards*. We were able to match the photographs we took of Snipiskiu in 2000 with those taken a century previously.

There are a few stairs at the level of the Planetarium and then a lot more stairs adjacent to St. Raphael. Three elevated box-enclosed flowerbeds separate the levels of stairs. There is a small garden at street level in front of the church.

I can conclude this verbal walking tour by mentioning that Snipiskiu *Gatve* widens as it slopes toward the Green Bridge. Herds of tourists going in opposite directions could pass without anyone brushing shoulders. Snipiskiu is also graded, with the intersection at Kalvariju considerably lower than where the hotel stands.

LOST AND FOUND IN PENSACOLA

Pensacola—June, 2001

June 25

The trip to Pensacola we took with Felicia Ford, her son Luke, and the six members of the Pecoraro family commenced from Philadelphia International Airport. The airport is just over seventy five miles from Little Egg Harbor, approximately an hour-and-a-half drive along the Garden State Parkway and Atlantic City Expressway. Traffic was light, and we made it to the airport expeditiously, unlike the return trip, which took four extra hours on account of bad weather and bad traffic. But that's getting ahead of the story.

Our connecting flight was in Memphis, Tennessee, which was the headquarters of Elvis Presley. Whatever his current situation, the King of Rock and Roll is prominently featured in the gift shops in the airport.

On the way to the airport I teased seven-year-old Luke about the dangers of voodoo in New Orleans. I told Luke that the voodoo women who live there can turn children into changelings merely by touching them on the forelocks.

I told him to make sure no strange women touch him, since the witches can take his soul and substitute an imposter Luke for the real Luke, who they take to *the other place*, never to be seen again. I think I scared him a little—and made him think. He was trying to figure out just what the heck changelings are and how it's possible to substitute one for a human soul. Smart boy that he is, he asked whether I was the real Dennis or an imposter Dennis. I told him I'm pretty sure I remember being the real Dennis, but that I couldn't be absolutely certain in these matters. After all, if witches can steal your soul and replace it with something else, they might also be able to supply a lifetime of fabricated memories.

I also teased Luke by giving him a list of safety regulations. (I got all but the last off the Pensacola Web site.) I told him never to swim alone. And that he has to wear sunscreen at all times. And to watch out for jellyfish. And to never touch jellyfish, even those that are playing possum on the shore, since they can be the notorious man-of-war species we learn about on the educational networks. And I told him that he has to cross the street in the event he spots an alligator standing on the corner.

I should have mentioned sharks. The week after we arrived home, there was a brutal shark attack on an eight-year-old boy in the waters off Fort Pickens beach.

Talk about scaring people. Just as the plane was lifting off the runway, Felicia questioned me about my beliefs about the afterlife. She asked whether or not I believe there's life after death or whether I believe death is extinction. Exactly the topics a person prefers to discuss as a plane takes off.

Felicia got off an unintentionally hilarious line as the plane started its descent—downward is a direction I feel mostly in the ears. She observed, rather loudly, that *the plane is going down*. She meant to say that the plane was *landing*. I don't think the people who heard her—nearly everyone in coach—wanted to hear the particular phrase *the plane is going down*. But no one panicked. Everyone knew what Felicia meant, which is proof that we ordinarily hear the meanings of words rather than the words themselves.

Jason, Ginny, and Shane York met us at the airport. (Ginny's sister, Julie, was there, too.) They look really great—I hope they feel as good as they look. Jason still looks young. It's hard to believe he's twenty six. Let's see, that makes me—I hate to think how old that makes me. Jason's a solid 210 pounds, but trim and buff, like the athlete he is. Ginny looks equally great, although she's not nearly as buff. She's six months pregnant, but still thin and hardly showing. Mothers tend to put on weight in the last trimester, so Ginny will look different in September than she does in June. This is something for her to look forward to.

The center of attention, of course, was Shane, at two-and-a-half years a handsome and intelligent little boy. Despite the number of people fighting among themselves for the chance to carry him, he wasn't the least bit shy. It's funny, but Shane looks like Ginny from the front and like Jason from the behind. He definitely resembles Ginny facially. Seeing Shane playing in the water later in the week reminded me of Jason when he was that age—twenty three years ago!

What strikes me about Shane is how verbal he is. He talks in long phrases that are grammatically correct. He's entering the "Why?" stage, which is delightful to hear. Of course, we saw him only for a week. But a child asking, "Why, Mommy?" and, "Why, Daddy?" and, "Why?" and, "Why?" and, "Why, and why?" allows us staid adults to revisit things about the world we stopped noticing. Being with a child asking, "Why, and why?" gives us the chance to become mentally young again.

I had a pleasant session with Shane later in the week. I asked what his name was and he said, "Shane." I asked what his doggie's name was and he said, "Angel." I asked what my name was and he said, "Uncle Dennis." (He pronounces it "Dinnis".) I asked what his mommy's name was and he said, "Mommy." I asked what his daddy's name was and he said, "Daddy." Right on all counts.

Pensacola has been on the map for four centuries. The original conquistadors were led by Don Tristan de Luna, who arrived on what is now Pensacola Beach with eleven ships in 1559. They were greeted by the *Panzacola* Indians, who belonged to the Choctaw tribe. The original Spanish didn't fare too well. Their colony was aborted three years later, owing to storms and to the failure of supply ships to reach them.

A second wave of conquistadors arrived in 1698 and established a successful colony on the site of the Naval Air Station. The Station itself started as a naval yard in 1825.

Since the time of Don Tristan, Pensacola has changed national identities several times. It has been claimed by Spain, France, Britain, the United States, and the Confederate States. Hence, the title, "City of Five Flags." There would have been six flags had the Panzacola flown one. "City of Five Flags and a Headdress" just doesn't make the cut of mottos.

Pensacola is a generic city. It looks like everyplace else and can be anywhere else in the United States. It doesn't look particularly *Southern*, despite the occasional palm tree and the enormous number of Protestant churches. The only distinguishing *Southern* landmark I noticed is rather astonishing. It's a large monument to "Our Confederate Dead" located on

West 98 in the heart of the business district. This monument stands on an island in the middle of the traffic—Route 98 is one of the main roads in town. It's quite tall, with a life-size gold-plated sculpture of a soldier at the top. The monument looks well maintained, the gold shiny brilliant, the grass on the median properly manicured and trimmed with flowers. The only thing missing was the word *Beloved* on the plaque.

As far as I can tell, there are three sections to the city. The section furthest from the wonderful Gulf beaches is stereotypically suburban. The airport is located in this section, amid vast stretches of shopping malls and apartment complexes. Davis Blvd., on which we had the pleasure of driving for an hour the day we got lost, is one continuous mall with only an occasional church or used car dealership to break up the retail monotony. Literally, every chain store in Bergen County, New Jersey, is represented in this stretch of Pensacola.

The business district is architecturally nondescript and marked for consideration only by the absence of tall buildings and pedestrians. The buildings are rarely more than four or five stories high; I wonder whether the threat of hurricanes has anything to do with keeping them on the small scale. What is striking, apart from the sawed-off architecture, is the emptiness of the streets. I saw very few pedestrians on our rides through the district. It's as if no one walks anywhere, and maybe there's nothing to walk to. I suppose everyone's at the beach when they're not in their offices.

The third section of Pensacola is nearest the Naval Air Station and the Gulf. I wish I could say it was particularly desolate and wild, but I can't. The section is speckled with creeks and dense with maritime forest—in places the growth is so profuse, you can't see the bark of the trees—but it's no more desolate and wild than the Pine Barrens I drive through three hundred days a year. There are more open spaces in this section of Pensacola than in the other two, many carpeted with lush grass and dotted with tangled copses, but there is also considerable construction going on. Just like in the disappearing maritime forests of Ocean County, New Jersey.

We stayed at a Comfort Inn. Three adjacent rooms on the first floor. The air conditioning worked fine, although the flow of air caught the drape and lifted it up and outward. I had to keep a piece of luggage against the drape to keep the cool air from being trapped. There was a safe, useful for our valuables, and a tiny refrigerator, useful for my beer, which is always Corona on vacations. The motel offered a buffet breakfast—bagels, bananas, and donuts—and, best of all, free coffee all hours of the day and night.

The pool was outside and secluded from the street by a tall, orange-shaded wall. Jason and the kids had a ball. Jason threw Matthew Pecoraro and Luke like he used to throw running backs in scrimmages. And Shane loved mixing it up with the boys. He was a minnow among marlins, but he was game. I took a lot of pictures of the kids playing in the pool. Unfortunately, none was of expert quality, since the camera wasn't the most sensitive and everyone was jumping, diving, swimming, and horsing around. The camera couldn't catch flying fish.

June 26

Our first full day in Pensacola began auspiciously. I happened to be standing at the window, admiring the sights—the parking lot—when Jennie Pecoraro passed by, walking rapidly and crying. She had been chased by a dog during her morning jog. She must have tried to outrun the dog, so it kept chasing her till a local resident intervened and came to the rescue. (I should have added "Watch out for the dogs" when I went through the list with Luke in the car on the way to the airport.) Fortunately, Jennie wasn't scratched or bitten and the incident soon passed.

Led by Jason, who horsed around roughly, the kids played in the pool for a few hours. We then drove to the Naval Aviation Museum, which is in the Naval Air Station about a half hour from the motel. The museum is within sight of the Pensacola Lighthouse. It's possible to climb to the top of the lighthouse, but we didn't get the chance, which is a shame. The lighthouse is reputed to be haunted. Specters have been seen on the staircase and there's a blood stain that reputedly never washes out on the floor of the keeper's shanty.

We watched a brief movie on the Blue Angels, the navy stunt pilots who travel the aviation circuit on what is, essentially, a propaganda campaign for the service. "Sign up today, boys, and you can fly one of these tomorrow!" The movie was on an IMAX screen the size of a building and had deafening sound effects.

After the movie I took Matthew and Luke in a flight simulator—this resembled the rides on the Boardwalk in Wildwood. The building moves in accordance with the film, so you have the physical illusion of doing what you see on screen. In this case, going on a bombing mission to an unnamed Middle Eastern country—we can guess which. I'm happy to report our mission ended successfully.

This flight simulator is about as close to real combat as I'll get, which is probably a good thing for the United States. And it was as close to riding in real military equipment. Jason was unable to get me a ride in the cabin of a nuclear submarine, like I had requested. I told him I wouldn't touch anything, especially the big red button marked "XXX", and it's well known I keep my promises.

Afterward, we viewed the various aircraft and toured a nice exhibit on Pensacola during the Second World War. Things were quaint then and a lot cheaper. I think Babci enjoyed this part of the museum. She's a member of "The Greatest Generation" and the exhibit was quite authentic, even to the extent of a bread odor in the kitchen. However, there was no beer at five cents a glass, as advertised.

We then drove to Fort Barrancas, which is located a few miles from the museum. This was one of three forts that defended Pensacola in the long ago. Fort Pickens stands near the tip of Pensacola Beach; we visited there later in the week. Fort McRee once stood on a barrier island across from Fort Pickens, but it has gone the way of Tucker's Island here in Little Egg Bay; that is, it has gone underwater.

The British built the first fort on this site in 1763. The Spanish, who captured this part of Florida in 1797, built a larger fort. America got the fort and Florida, too, from Spain in 1819.

Barrancas and the other forts served well in the age of wooden vessels. Their cannons could sink defenseless ships and the weaponry on the ships could do little damage to the massive walls of the forts. This changed when ironclads emerged during the Civil War. Metal vessels matched the firepower of the forts and were as thickly shielded. Because of these changes in weaponry, Barrancas slowly drifted into obscurity. After the Civil War it served as a training ground, a signal station, and a storage depot. It was restored in the 1970s as part of the national park system. Much of the brickwork visible on the exterior of the fort dates only from the 1970s.

I wrote that Barrancas slowly drifted into obscurity, but it and Fort Pickens could have played greater roles in America's history if the Dark Lords who write the scripts plotted the mayhem differently. Barrancas has a claim to having fired the first shots of the Civil War. And Pickens missed replacing Fort Sumter in our nation's history by only a few days.

On January 7, 1861, a full three months before the events in Charleston, Company G of the First U.S. Artillery fired at unknown assailants of the Secesh type who tried to attack the fort. Three days later, Lt. Adam Slemmer, who commanded Company G, fled across the bay to Fort Pickens, a more secure base.

There was a gradual build up of troops on both sides for the next three months. Braxton Bragg, commander in Pensacola and later a full Confederate general, exhibited his astonishing ineptness for the first time in what became the War Between the States; greater exhibitions of ineptitude would follow. An attack planned for April 9 went awry, since supplies for the attack had not arrived and the element of surprise was lost when a traitor was identified.

Before the attack could be carried out, Fort Sumter swiped the spotlight of history.

Our tour of Barrancas began at a well-stocked bookstore and visitor center. From the store a trail leads gently upwards to the fort. The fort itself looks to be divided in two sections. The more northerly, and impressive, portion is a roughly triangular building. This portion cleverly followed the contour of the land and was hidden from view until we reached the brow of the trail. The southern portion of the fort is lunette in shape and sits on the edge of a bluff overlooking Pensacola Bay. (*Barrancas* is Spanish for *bluff*.) At the base of the bluff is a heavily traveled road—there is no confusion over which century is open for view. There's an open field between portions of the fort. Possibly the field served as a parade ground.

A surprising feature is how distant the fort is from the water. There must have been considerable changes in terrain over the years.

Access to the northern portion of the fort is through a drawbridge raised about ten feet over a dry moat. The brickwork of the fort is dark orange or light red. The walls are said to be four feet thick.

The most impressive features of Fort Barrancas are the scarp galleries. These are cramped passageways that run along the outer walls of the fort. Every few feet narrow triangular windows open to the exterior. In Lt. Slemmer's time these windows would have been manned by infantry. In our time the only shots from these windows fire from the shutters of digital cameras.

The scarps are dark, damp, musty, and littered with graffiti. And they are eerie places. Babci, who ventured in the galleries with Luke, said they reminded her of the KGB cells we visited in Vilnius in June, 1997. I don't think the comparison was far off visually, although Barrancas hasn't nearly so bleak a history.

The athletes that we are, Jennie and I decided to walk the complete scarp. Everyone else took the direct path that led into bright sunshine. The galleries consist of a number of long passages connected at right angles. Each passage goes on for quite a distance—you make a sharp turn expecting to emerge from the fort and another long passage opens up, gloomier than the previous one. About halfway in, we weren't sure how many turns were left—or whether we had taken a wrong turn.

As we went round and round inside the gloomy tunnels I teased Jennie about sensing paranormal influences and about the galleries being haunted. It was, after all, a place that had seen combat. It was a place where men may have died. I told Jennie that I felt a presence following us and that I felt *creeped out*, like I was being watched from *the ethereal world*. I think I scared her a little and I think I was scared a little, too. I preferred not to turn around to see if I were, in fact, a sensitive and spoke correctly. I'm not endowed with supernatural talents—I'm not endowed with natural talents either—but sometimes you hit it right on your first foray into the great beyond. There was no slaughter in the fort, but who's to say some young soldier far from home didn't die tragically in one of these passages? Who's to say a young lad didn't accidentally shoot himself while standing watch where we walked? And who's to say another man didn't die of a childhood disease while standing picket duty for his country? For being imaginary, these were very real possibilities.

Talk about taking a wrong turn!

We came to the crossroad of our lives in rush hour traffic in the heart of the Pensacola business district. It was an existential moment of choice—continue driving or make a right turn. We were separated from Jason and Joe Pecoraro by several cars, so I couldn't see their choices. The traffic was abnormally heavy—literally, the circus was in town and elephants were on the roads. I had to make up my mind in a hurry—that's the one thing I can't do is make up my mind in a hurry. At the last second I chose to turn right, and it was the wrong road taken.

The right turn led to Route 110, which is the way we were supposed to go. But Route 110 soon divides, west toward Mobile, east toward Tallahassee. I wasn't sure which way to turn at this crossroad, so I chose to turn right again—Tallahassee sounded less ominous than Mobile and the signs pointed toward the airport. It was, of course, the wrong turn.

There's nothing more maddening than being lost in the middle of a major city. We were on heavily-traveled Davis Blvd. in the midst of an endless stream of malls, Protestant churches, and used car dealerships, and it was the wrong place to be. We went round and round, up one way on Davis Blvd. and then down another way. We went round and round, up one side street and then down another side street. I left my cell phone in the motel, I didn't have Jason's home phone number, for the first time in my life I didn't have a pen and, worst of all, I didn't know the address of the Comfort Inn. It was another fine mess, compounded by the fact that no one knew where anything was. Convenience store clerks were mostly Orientals; they weren't sure where they were, still less where we were. Gas station attendants spoke English, but confused the Comfort Inn with the Holiday Inn. Twice, they sent us in the wrong direction. After an hour of futile driving, we pulled into a Texaco station run by a tiny elderly lady. When I told her I didn't know where I was or where the motel was, she promptly whipped out a phone book and cell phone from under the counter and called the first Comfort Inn she saw listed. After she confirmed with the desk clerk that there was a guest with the surname *Ford*, she gave us perfect directions. Turns out we should have taken the road that led toward Mobile. All it cost to get back to the motel was three dollars for candy and soda, since we didn't need gas. This kind lady was incredibly helpful. About the only thing she didn't do was say, "This sort of thing happens all the time." I would have felt a little better if she had.

June 27

Today we went to New Orleans.

We chose to use two cars rather than three, which meant that I got the chance to sightsee (and not to get lost). It took a bit of work sorting out who was going with whom, since the kids had to stay with their respective mothers and everyone wanted to ride with Shane.

The trip was two hundred miles each way or three-and-a-half hours. It would have been longer if I drove.

The trip was mostly on Interstate 10. The posted speed was seventy-five miles an hour, which meant eighty-five miles an hour. For most of the trip the scenery was bland and reminded me of the Pine Barrens—it was maritime forest with an occasional parting of the woods for a peek at wetlands and creeks. The interstate crosses two impressive bodies of water—the Gulf of Mobile and Lake Pontchartrain outside New Orleans. Both bodies are very broad and both are traversed by low bridges that run for miles.

The battleship USS *Alabama* lies in Mobile harbor near the highway. The guns are clearly visible and are trained over the road. The ship stands out against the flat city—only a few tall buildings are visible—and is especially impressive at night, when its silhouette is brilliantly illuminated.

Lake Pontchartrain is very blue and was easily the most picturesque part of the trip. On the return to Pensacola we stopped for gas at a remote place called the Irish Bayou. The lake came almost to the shores of the gas station—it was a tranquil and appealing setting. I felt like I wanted to linger to savor and memorize the beauty, but we had time only to grab some snacks and "fill-'er-up". An unusual white edifice consisting of what looked to be one part castle, another part church, stood south of the gas station. I have no idea what this building was—it seemed an obscure and forbidding structure.

A surprising sight in Mississippi was the excessive number of billboards along the highway. There must have been a hundred in bunches of fives. Most of the billboards advertised the gambling casinos in Biloxi. Atlantic City style gambling appears to be the fad in the land of mint juleps and magnolias, and it is pushed mightily. Lady Bird Johnson must be ashamed.

New Orleans was not as impressive as I anticipated. The tourist section reminded me of St. Mark's Place in Manhattan, but without the crowds. I imagine it must be a happening place for young people and for single people, what with all the clubs, taverns, and girlie bars, but it doesn't seem the place to tour with a family or with young children.

Joe and Jason parked in a garage on St. Anne Street, which was located close to the Mississippi and to the famous bars and restaurants. On the building next to the garage a plaque informed us that the first school in New Orleans was founded on the site in the eighteenth century. Another schoolhouse and another plaque were in the direction of Bourbon Street. This plaque warned that it is a serious offense to bring guns into the schoolhouse.

As we walked toward the river St. Anne's Church was on the right near a park. Like its sister church in Vilnius, St. Anne's is one of the most famous structures in New Orleans. It is featured in innumerable paintings and prints in art shops. The park was on the grunge side, inhabited mostly by old people—they are left out of the artwork. At the outskirts of the park were tables populated by psychics of varying talents. Felicia and Kim Pecoraro sat for readings on the way home. Their prospects appear good, so their psychic must have been one of the ones with talent.

St. Anne's St. concludes at Decatur Ave., one of the famous drags in town. Du Monde's Coffee and Bakery Shop is at the intersection. Du Monde's is famous for the *beignet*, a flat zeppoli whose praises are sung across the globe, mostly by people from New Orleans. Du Monde's is also famous for their coffee, but I found it flat and tasteless. The French Market is a few blocks from Du Monde's on Decatur. It's a well-known destination, but it amounted to an overcrowded and overpriced flea market. Little alligator heads and hot sauces were featured. The alligator heads were artificial, the sauces were real. So were the singe marks in my throat.

A terrific thunderstorm broke out when we left the French Market. Kathy Pecoraro bought everyone ponchos, which allowed us to walk in the rain and awful humidity. Babci is still a great trooper able to make a day-long trek at the age of—well, we don't want to know her age, and she won't say it. Our destination was Bourbon St. in general and some famous restaurant in particular. We found the former in no time; the latter took more walking.

Bourbon St. is a strange mixture of seedy and slick, second-rate and classy. A go-go bar stands across the street from a five-star hotel. A hole-in-the-wall sells hot dogs with chili sauce across the street from a five-star restaurant. A dive pours flat beer from rusty faucets across the street from a bar slipping X/O cognac out of green bottles. In places I felt like I had been transported back in time to the heyday of raunch in Midtown Manhattan. There were a number of topless joints and strip clubs, all with gaudy entrances and disreputable characters touting the action inside. Like I said, this was not the place for children.

There were quite a number of intoxicated people on the streets—this was mid-afternoon. One wino actually started to sing, "The Big Easy, The Big Easy" when he saw us pass.

I don't know what the style of architecture is called, but it's exactly what appears in postcards. The houses are wood, two and three stories high, brightly painted, and heavily fronted with terraces, verandahs, and shutters. The houses on the side streets are covered with ivy and frequently sit behind courtyards overgrown with lush vegetation. The buildings take up most of the sidewalks; on some blocks, only one person at a time can pass.

Finding a restaurant in this city of restaurants is surprisingly not easy, especially for a group of fourteen, all with particular tastes. Hunger was making everyone cranky. The heavy rain didn't help our moods. Nor did the fact that we were dressed like the Klan—we weren't sure how this would play in a city that looked to have as many *brothers* as *rednecks*.

Jennie led us around till we reached Pat O'Brien's, an upscale restaurant where she ate when she visited New Orleans on a previous trip. Half of Pat O'Brien's is outdoors and the half that was indoors was so highly air-conditioned it was impossible to sit without forming icicles. It didn't make sense to pay top dollar to be squeezed under umbrellas in the pouring rain just to say we ate at Pat O'Brien's, so we moved on and found a restaurant that was indoors and dry and sufficiently atmospheric to be in The Big Easy. It was called Jumbo's—a lot of things in New Orleans are called *Jumbo's*. I had rice and beans and two Dixie beers, a local beverage that was light in color and easy going down. The rest of the folks had jumbo-sized dinners but no beer. Matthew had filet mignon and Babci and Kathy had a fishy soup. I didn't see any of the famous Louisiana crawfish doing the breaststroke in the soup, but the broth was thick and, truth to tell, I didn't want to look too closely. My vegan soul shouldn't have to see such sights as swimming crawfish.

After dinner we proceeded toward the Riverwalk and the Mississippi River. The walk was a healthy hike, meandering through a generic business district—the district contained a colorful trolley line and a few undistinguished skyscrapers. On the way Danielle Pecoraro asked a street musician if he knew any B.B. King. He did, changing on the instant from a guitar to a harmonica. He took it in stride and played a few notes, although he must have been surprised that Danielle, a white teenager from New Jersey, requested B.B. King on the streets of The Big Easy. Quite a touching moment.

Like everything else in New Orleans, the Riverwalk is overrated. It commences at an aquarium, which is a huge glass building that looks wet from the outside, and concludes at Du Monde's. We took some pictures near a fountain and the kids had ice cream. There are several ferries that dock along the Riverwalk near the aquarium. There was also a picturesque riverboat replete with huge red paddles.

The area around the ferry landings didn't look to be the safest. There were several shady-looking teenagers hanging around the fountain and an elderly intoxicated man strolled from bench to bench singing for donations. I think Jennie sent him off with the half-excuse that we were on a family reunion and preferred to talk among ourselves than to hear an off-key version of "The Saints Come Marching In."

The Mississippi is America's great river—the *Father of Waters*, Lincoln called it—and I don't doubt that it is. But the river is unimpressive in this part of town. We might call it the *Son* or *Grandson of the Father of Waters*. It's maybe a quarter-mile wide and restrained by bland bulkheads overbuilt to the high-water mark with apartment buildings and office complexes. A bridge crosses farther downstream—the structure is a simple steel frame. I imagined the Mississippi a roaring, raging, brown god sweeping everything in its path and spilling over and drowning the countryside. (That's on its good days.) I'm sure it does these things, but it was tranquil on the day we visited, and I suppose we should count ourselves lucky.

By the time we circled round to St. Anne's everything had fallen apart. I bought coffee and *beignets* from a disagreeable waitress at Du Monde's. Kathy and Jennifer ran to do last-minute shopping. Felicia and Kim consulted a psychic. Joe took the kids to get balloons from a vendor who talked about Jesus and the high rents in town—the vendor was sure Jesus wouldn't charge such high rents if he were a landlord. Jason and Ginny were getting edgy, so they crossed the street and waited in the shade. Shane was in his carriage. He was either awake or asleep, I forget which; if he was awake, he would have been cranky. Babci was definitely cranky, and she had a right to be, given her heroic march through the Big Easy at the ripe age of—well, I never found out.

The trip back to Pensacola was easy. We stopped at the Irish Bayou around 7:30 PM. I bought "Ozarka" bottled water—my Jersey accent didn't change when I ordered it. About an hour later, we stopped at a roadside rest stop in Mississippi. Everyone rushed for the rest rooms and for the snack machines, which were securely tucked behind huge metal gratings. Our visit was cut short by the diversity of insect life that found a liking for fine Yankee examples of the human species.

June 28

Today we went to the beach.

Before we left I got off some jokes to the kids about whether they *hablando Espanol*. When they inquired why they needed to know Spanish, I told them that, if they got caught in it, the undertow will take them straight to Mexico. I advised them to say when they arrived, *"Mi nombre es Matthew Pecoraro"* and *"My madre es Kathleen y mi padre es Jose."* They are to remember to praise Pancho Villa, curse General Pershing, and never use the word "stinking" except in the same phrase as *"Estados Unidos"*. They should use the words *"amigo y amiga"* a lot and they should mention that, since they are in Mexico, they would like to visit the shrine of Our Lady of Guadalupe.

I joked about the undertow because Jason mentioned it on several occasions. The Gulf is rougher than our gentle New Jersey ocean and six people drowned in Pensacola waters the week before we arrived due to tropical storm Allison.

The trip to the beach is made along Route 98. The ride—a half hour when the driver is not lost—crosses Pensacola Bay on two bridges. The first is called "Three Mile Bridge". This connects the business section of Pensacola with Gulf Breeze, an upscale community on the tip of the long peninsula that juts into the sound. The road curves eastward at this point and continues inland—later in the week we drove it some thirty miles to get to the aquarium in Fort Walton.

The second bridge, called "One Mile Bridge", connects Gulf Breeze with Pensacola Beach, a spit of a barrier island that runs for miles. The island doesn't appear to be more than a half mile wide in places. I would hate to be on it during a storm; I'm not sure anyone could be on it during a storm. Fort Pickens stands at the westernmost tip. Since we never drove in that direction, I'm not sure what stands at the easternmost tip. I'm sure it's something equally wonderful.

There's a toll near the entrance of the island—for a moment, I thought we were in New Jersey. Beyond the toll is a small esplanade called The Boardwalk, which contains gift stores, bars, and fast food restaurants. The Boardwalk is sufficiently overrated to be housed along the Mississippi in New Orleans. But the bay that opens behind the shops is expansive and picturesque. I took a few pictures of the water, with vast cumulus clouds in the distance and a hot-air balloon in the foreground.

There are a number of hotels and condo complexes clustered around The Boardwalk. They stretch for a few miles on either side of the road. The rest of the island is quite desolate. The dunes on the ocean side are very tall in places, causing a slight tilt in perception.

The beach is narrow. The sand is perfectly white but rough on the soles—this must indicate it's a new beach. The water is clear and bathtub warm and bright green in appearance close to the shore—it turns blue farther out. The water is rough with a strong pull that grabs you and doesn't let go. Surprisingly, there's little surf. The water just heaves in and out without generating a lot of waves.

One heave almost took Babci out, who slipped going in. It was a nerve-wracking initiation to the Gulf of Mexico. Poor Babci would have had a difficult time in Mexico, since she doesn't know Spanish and they don't know Polish, and she probably would have asked to visit the Shrine of Our Lady of Czestochowa, which would be insulting to the *ghente*.

Everyone loved the water, but we left after an hour and drove to a beach on the bay side. It was safer there—no grabbing and no heaving. Matthew and Luke played fantasy-action games in the water for two hours without interruption. Babci, Danielle, and I baby sat Shane, which really meant following him around the shallow water making sure he didn't fall and go under. Jason, Ginny, and Kim went jet skiing. They had some serious falls, which leads to this interesting question—Jason can rescue the girls, if need be, since he's a strong swimmer, but what happens when a rescue swimmer needs rescue?

The water in the bay was calm and shallow. It was also typically slimy, with lots of seaweed and schools of invisible fish nibbling our feet. These fish are the aquatic version of sea-me-gnats. I don't know how the children didn't feel the nibbling—I didn't think I was having a tactile hallucination. Probably, they were too busy playing.

That evening we dined at a Crackerjack restaurant. This is a chain of restaurants that features home-style cooking and a gift shop loaded with expensive treats. The service is slow, which allows for more time in the gift shop. But I have no complaints once we got served. I had a selection of hearty vegetable dishes, including macaroni-and-cheese, which qualifies as a vegetable in this part of the world.

Later that evening we visited Sam's Amusement Park. Sam's is touted on the Pensacola Web site, a situation that invites the issue of truth-in-advertising. It's clean, spotlessly so, and on a small scale, probably with less than fifteen attractions. (The park closed an hour after our arrival, so we really didn't get to ride on many.) Sam's has the strangest pricing scheme I've ever encountered in an amusement park. Rides are priced differently, which makes buying coupon books difficult. Rides are also assigned to different categories. The scheme is so complex, the operators are as confused as the customers. In one case the lady working the ride took the wrong category of tickets, leaving us short when we wanted to go on another ride. To balance things out, another operator took a lower-priced ticket than the one she was supposed to.

Things are going to become more confused in the future because Sam advertised expansions in the coming seasons. Customers are going to need graduate degrees to figure out differences in prices between kids' rides and rides for grown-up kids at heart.

June 29

This was a day of highs and lows and bad weather and changeable moods.

We drove to the Picture Perfect Photography Studio to take our family portrait. The studio was run by a lady named Paula and was located on a farm somewhere in the Pensacola outlands. There were roosters, geese, dogs, box turtles, and a healthy animal odor on her property. We took six pictures, as I recall. I liked one in particular, which presently hangs on the foyer wall.

We then drove to the Yorks' apartment in the Northwood complex on East Olive Drive. It was quite close to where we were lost the other day; in fact, we crossed East Olive Drive several times on our impromptu tour of Davis Blvd. Their apartment was small and cozy. Shane's room was loaded with toys and the living room was loaded with photographs of Shane. Everyone met Angel, their beautiful black dog. Angel came to each of us in turn to sniff and be petted and then immediately circled back to Jason. Unfortunately, she is ill of late, suffering seizures.

I tried to record Shane on the camcorder, but got only a half hour's worth of film. Later, we walked outside and I filmed for a little longer. But it started to rain, so our walk was cut short.

I've since kidded Jason that Pensacola is the rain capital of the world. Whenever I check the Weather Channel, Pensacola is covered with clouds and rain—drownpours, usually—is in the forecast. As we experienced on our visit, the rain is tropical in nature. This means it's torrential when it comes, with abrupt starts and stops and a constant humidity hovering near three digits.

I found out after we returned to New Jersey that Felicia sensed a ghostly presence in their apartment. I myself felt no paranormal influences, but I'm not gifted that way.

We then drove to visit the row of shops on the bayside of Pensacola Beach—this is the aforementioned Boardwalk. The visit was marred by the second major controversy of our trip. Everyone was in a frazzled mood by now—I know I get edgy if I have to act pleasantly for too long—and I got lost for the second time. This is not good for my reputation.

There's no shame in making a mistake. The only shame is having to admit you made one. But I have to be honest. I'm without fault here, as I am in most things. Jason made the mistake. He said *East 98* when he meant *West 98*. I know it doesn't sound like much, but there is a *big* difference. West 98 leads to the wonderful Gulf beaches. East 98 leads to the edge of one's nerves.

I had the same perplexing experience as on our repetitious excursions on Davis Blvd. No one knew where anything was, except for one sensible lady who told us to go back in the opposite direction. By the time she suggested this I was so thoroughly lost I didn't know where the opposite direction was. I was speaking English in America and not getting my meaning across. It can't be too difficult answering, "How do I get from the spot I am standing on to the beach?" For a moment I thought I was speaking English in Lithuania. I think I would have found my way easier in Lithuania.

About the only pleasant aspect of our ten-mile detour was passing the motel I stayed in when I visited Jason in June, 1994. I remember that I read some Kennedy Assassination literature when I waited for him to arrive. That was the day of the O.J. Simpson Bronco chase. I remember we watched the chase that evening and wondered whether O.J. would commit suicide. I predicted he would. Like I say, I hardly ever make a mistake.

Everyone was annoyed when we finally arrived at The Boardwalk an hour late. We were annoyed for being lost. They were annoyed that we got lost. And nothing was worth getting lost over. The stores on The Boardwalk were major disappointments, although I did buy a replica of the Pensacola Lighthouse and a few decorative stones for the front of our house. We went our separate ways after a snack in a pizzeria. Joe, Kathy, and Felicia went back to the Comfort Inn, Jason and Ginny went back to their haunted apartment on East Olive Dr., and Babci and I went to Fort Pickens. We got the best deal. Fort Pickens was the historical highlight of the trip.

Fort Pickens is the name of the actual fort and of the surrounding national park. The park contains campgrounds, a nature walk, a fishing pier on the bayside, and a number of unguarded ocean beaches. The beaches are beautiful, but lonely. One was the site of a ferocious shark attack that occurred the week after we returned to New Jersey. An eight-year-old boy was savagely mauled by a shark. The boy survived the attack, but his recovery will be long and, sad to relate, not fully complete.

The fort stands on the western tip of Pensacola Beach. The land has changed quite a bit, so the fort is no longer at the water's edge, but some ways inland. East of the fort are two huge World War Two redoubts—the Langhon redoubts. These are immense concrete bunkers several stories tall and heavily overgrown with foliage.

There was a Civil War battle about a mile east of the fort. On the night of October 9, 1861, Braxton Bragg sent a raiding party onto Pensacola Beach. The putative objective was the capture of Fort Pickens, but like everything Bragg did in the war, the battle turned into confusion and into defeat. Initial Confederate success in overrunning green Yankee troops led to the disorganization of victory and into a reversal. Equally green in combat experience and uniquely led by the luminous bumbler Bragg, the Southrons withdrew at a cost of eighteen killed. The Federals suffered fourteen dead, but held onto Pickens, which remained in Union hands throughout the war.

The Federal troops engaged in the battle were the Sixth New York Regiment—Wilson's Zouaves. They were mostly Irish immigrants from the Bowery District of Manhattan. Their reputation as fighters was not as good as their reputation for carousing under the influence.

Fort Pickens opened in 1834 and functioned in some capacity into the 1940s. It consisted of over twenty million bricks manufactured locally. Much of the construction was done using slave labor. The initial structure was pentagonal in shape, with gun batteries or bastions at each of the corners. The present fort contains four walls. The fifth bastion blew heavenward in 1899 when stored gunpowder accidentally discharged. The absent wall allows free access into the central parade ground. In the old days, when the absent wall was present, the entrance would have been through large oak doors located above a moat. Just like in the movies.

The interior of the fort has undergone considerable change since 1834. Rooms have been added and deleted—Geronimo, the famous Apache warrior, stayed under house arrest in one of the rooms in the 1880s. The major change was the addition of an elevated gun battery in the middle of the parade ground in 1898.

The intact portions of the fort consist of long passages that are much wider than the ones in Barrancas. Two of the bastions held tunnels loaded with stockpiles of gunpowder. Two weeks' worth, or two hundred fifty thousand pounds, was always on hand.

The western bastion is the oldest surviving portion of the fort. The climb to the top was not easy. The stairs are narrow and steep, but Babci took them like the old trooper she is—trooper, anyway. A fifteen-inch Rodman gun, an immense black rhino of a weapon, stands atop the bastion. The barrel, which is raised high over the platform, is something like ten feet long. Huge, inert, inoperative, the gun is intimidating even in repose. Its targets are less challenging in this century than in the Civil War era—just a few beach shanties and dilapidated World War Two barracks in the nearby sand and weeds.

I'm proud to say we returned to the Comfort Inn without getting lost. On the trip back we passed the beach where Jason and I swam when I came to Pensacola the first time. The area is more developed than I remembered, but I recognized the roadside shelter where we took snapshots.

That evening, our party scattered. I took Felicia, Ginny, and the kids to the Barnes & Noble on Airport Road so everyone could buy a book.

Afterward, we stopped in the International House of Pancakes for dinner. The food was fine, but the service was deplorable. It seems everyone in this region of Pensacola stopped in for late dinner. Shane slept throughout the ordeal, which was an undisguised blessing.

Joe and everyone else traveled to Biloxi, Mississippi, to gamble. Everyone lost except for Kathy—or for me, since I gave her a few bucks to place a bet, which turned out to be a hit. The payoff paid for our excursion to the aquarium the following day. I think one of the delightful aspects of the trip was the fact that Sophia Ford, the great-granddaughter of Juozas Bielawski and Petronele Falkawska of Kalniskes village, Turgeli parish, Lithuania, spent a night of serious gambling in Biloxi, Mississippi, the home of Jefferson Davis, first and only president of the Confederate States of America.

June 30

Today started out with torrential rain. The interpersonal weather stayed stormy, too.

Everyone seemed depressed by the rain, the kind that looked like it wasn't going to let up. I managed to film for another half-hour—mostly Jason horsing around with the kids. It didn't look particularly rough while I was filming, but the film showed their play to be seriously, even dangerously, rough—it wasn't so much a fandango as a fandanger. Jason picked Luke up and threw him on the bed, and Luke pushed Matthew, and Shane pushed Luke, and the three scrambled to be the next one thrown.

While I was filming, there was an off-camera discussion about our activities for the day. The options were shopping or visiting an aquarium. The latter choice won out, which was the better option.

The drive took about forty five minutes on East 98. Like everything else in Pensacola, the road consisted of a repetitive two-sided procession of malls, Protestant churches, and used car dealerships. Except for the occasional palm tree and for breaks in the strip malls where the foamy gray ocean showed through, we could have been on Route 17 in Bergen County, New Jersey.

The aquarium was in Fort Walton Beach. It's called "Gulfarium" and advertises itself as the oldest "marine show" in the United States. It must also be among the priciest, with tickets going for $18.00 an adult. If Kathy didn't hit in Biloxi, admission would have broken the bank—or necessitated a swim to the nearest money machine.

Gulfarium consisted of a number of tanks with various marine attractions. The attractions couldn't be any wetter than we were—it poured continuously during our visit.

One tank held a number of sharks. We arrived just in time for feeding. This amounted to an attendant standing on the edge of the tank and dangling fish in the water. The sharks circled around and took the bait; they never took the hand that fed them. As they passed, the attendant stroked them. The feeding evoked no frenzy; to the contrary, everything proceeded in a docile and orderly fashion. The sharks slowly swam in single file and didn't seem particularly hungry, but then feeding happens several times a day. They don't know it, but those sharks were experiencing what we humans call "the good life". The only sinister element of the show was the distinctive snapping sounds the sharks' jaws made as they took the chum.

Another tank was a marine version of a petting zoo for children. This tank held a number of inert sea creatures—horseshoe crabs, clams, and starfish. Nothing that couldn't be found on the Jersey Shore. A sign requested that no specimen be lifted out of the water. The sign didn't faze the children. Except for the horseshoe crabs—they looked slightly intimidating—the creatures spent as much time out of the water as in it.

The main attractions, of course, were the dolphins. I've seen enough episodes of *Flipper* to appreciate their abilities. What struck me seeing them in the flesh was their size and grace. They were much larger than I anticipated.

We saw two shows. In one show the dolphins performed by their sleek selves. The highlight was a dolphin leaping some twenty or more feet out of the tank to grab a fish the handler held in her mouth; this was quite amazing and a tad disgusting. In the other show, billed as an "inter-species show", the dolphins interacted with sea lions. We also saw a show involving sea lions, creatures that seemed as intelligent as the dolphins and as large and graceful. The sea lions were related, being mothers, sisters, and daughters to one another; some were more than twenty years old. The male sea lions must have been out working.

Ginny, Shane, and I visited the fish tanks inside the main building. One tank held a puffer fish—this is the famous fish Japanese high rollers eat at risk to their lives. The puffer doesn't know this, but it is an ugly fish. It must taste a lot better than it looks. Another tank held a moray eel inserted among rocks. I'm sure the moray is a nasty creature in the wild, but this one looked rather elderly and out-of-aquatic-shape, laboriously raising and lowering its jaws as if it were struggling for breath. Shane seemed intrigued by these specimens as much as he had been by the acrobatic dolphins and sea lions. Our visit brought back memories of my trip to Oahu in 2000 when we watched the *"fishies"* in the ponds outside the flea market in Honolulu. The *fishies* were football-sized goldfish that did engage in feeding frenzies when tourists pitched leftovers into the pond. Compared to the lethargic sharks in Fort Walton, the goldfish were downright ferocious.

We stopped for supper at McGuire's Irish Pub, one of the premiere restaurants in Pensacola. McGuire's is located on an island on Route 98. I remembered it from my first visit. Strange to say, I remembered what we ate back then. Jason had steak and I had cherry beer, a local specialty, and a vegetable pizza that we took back to the motel where we watched the O.J. Simpson debacle play out on national television. For the life of me, I can't remember what I ate this trip. Whatever it was, I'm sure it tasted fine and came in obscenely large portions—everything in McGuire's comes in obscenely large portions.

McGuire's was jammed and exceedingly noisy with tourists and local yuppies—you couldn't hear yourself chew. A lot of drinking was going on amid all the eating, and there was a lot of eating going on. McGuire's is famous for a custom that has continued for two decades. Guests give money, which is then markered and tacked to the walls. One hundred thousand dollars hang from the woodwork. Quite an ambiance!

July 1

This was our day of departure. It turned out to be one of the longest days of our lives. It felt as if we spent nearly as much time departing as we spent visiting.

It started at the local Burger King, where we passed several hours drinking coffee and clogging our arteries with fries and donuts. Our intention was to go to a diner, but this was Sunday morning and all the people in Pensacola not in churches were in diners. The people not in diners were lined up outside diners.

On the way to the airport we ran into a road block—a freight train was rumbling across the direct route. We waited in traffic for a while—it seemed a long while—and then took a roundabout route. We got to the airport with time to spare, but we should have seen the delay as an omen of what was waiting.

Pensacola Airport is on the small scale and very user friendly. We checked in, returned the rentals—the miles I used up came from being lost—and sat around for a while. We took pictures, hugged, and said good-by several times.

As I wrote previously, Jason, Ginny, and Shane looked great—and their family looks different now. I am writing this on October 4, 2001. Two days ago, Ginny gave birth to Evan York, all of eight pounds and nine ounces. (A lineman, surely.) Evan is the first baby in our family group born in the twenty first century. Much to my distress, the world is growing increasingly remote from how it was when I was a child. Shane and Evan will grow up in a world that isn't as secure as we once thought. But they come from good people from as far back as I can trace and I feel certain they will be able to manage, whatever the future brings.

Every baby's birth allows us to think the world is starting over. In the middle of my life Evan gives me the feeling that the world has another chance.

The flight to Memphis was made in crystal clear skies. The plane circled, providing excellent views of the city below. I didn't see Elvis, but I did see the Mississippi as it ran its convoluted course. By this stage in its journey the river assumed its storybook persona—sinewy and sloppy and soupy brown. Seen from a thousand feet, its twisted, twisting path confirmed that the river—*the river*, I should write—carries the continent as it flows.

The first glance at the Departures Board caused more turbulence in our bellies than the flight from Pensacola. There were delays and cancellations throughout the Northeast, owing to a vast belt of thunderstorms. Newark, Kennedy, LaGuardia—Mother Nature was raising hell east of the Delaware. Philadelphia International was still open, leading to the hope that the storm had passed. But that hope didn't last. A red-faced Northwest Airlines attendant arrived and disclosed that the storms had just stopped flights in and out of the City of Brotherly Love. We would be delayed a half hour. This attendant returned after a half hour—his face was redder—and disclosed that we would be further delayed. At this news there was a gestural *"Oh No!"* among the crowd and a mass sinking of bodies on their chairs. Gravity suddenly became heavier.

The weather cleared after two hours of suffering the unnoticed effects of high blood pressure and we were promptly aloft. Strange as this is to say, there was a mad stampede among the planes to be first out of Memphis. I think we finished place or show.

The weather cleared over Philadelphia International and the planes descended—all of them at once. It was 10:00 PM and the airport was a madhouse, with hundreds of people rushing to the same destination—long-term parking.

Northwest Airlines did a commendable job keeping us informed about the weather, but the airport did a horrible job accommodating the scramble. Service to the parking lot amounted to a few buses running on a late-night schedule. The lines to the buses were a hundred people long and two hundred pieces of luggage deep. Joe and I left the luggage with Kathy, Felicia, and Babci, and hiked through the airport to try to get to the lot on foot, but that proved impossible. We just went round and round among the crowds. After touring the airport at a breakneck pace, we returned to the bus line. It was now two hundred people long and four hundred pieces of luggage deep.

I wish I could say the rest of the night went smoothly after we retrieved the cars, but it didn't. (It went worse for Joe and Kathy—it was their turn to get lost.) At 11:00 PM the traffic leading back to the airport was horrendous—it could not have been worse in the Holland Tunnel at rush hour. Ten lanes of traffic merged into one. The Northwest terminal was the end of the line, meaning we had to squeeze past delays at three other terminals and God knows how many carriers, each crowded to capacity. I was mighty tempted to leave everyone behind and drive home by myself, and I would have, too, if I could, but I doubt I would have made faster progress.

There are any number of signs leading to the airport. Leaving the airport, there's exactly one sign pointing to New Jersey, and it's crooked. After that, you're on your own. It's as if they don't want you to leave Pennsylvania. We stopped for directions at a convenience store somewhere near the border. I asked a Slavic-accented gentleman standing at the door how we could get to New Jersey. He said there were two ways, each leading over bridges. I said he should direct us to the nearest bridge.

Our vacation ended at 2:00 AM on July 2. I wasn't in a good mood the last leg of the journey—there isn't much to see along the Atlantic City Expressway at two in the afternoon, never mind at two in the morning. The weather was hot and humid; sealed for a week, the house was hotter and more humid. I was tired, my eyes were popping out of my head, and work was four hours away.

With a good night's rest and the settling back into the routine came an appreciation of our trip to Pensacola. We were together as a family—with fourteen people, there were bound to be disagreements. We made it back and forth without incident, even if the last leg of the return flight proved aggravating. I got to see Pensacola for the second time, I got to swim in the green Gulf, and I got to see two historical forts. And I got to see Jason, Ginny, and Shane. All in all, it was a good trip. God willing, we might try it again sometime.

A Pensa-coda

I think we left good feelings behind in Pensacola. I also left behind a paperback novel, *Other Worlds* by Barbara Michaels (Harper Collins, 2000). This was the first book by Barbara Michaels I had the pleasure of reading. I'm sure she commands a wide readership, but I regret to say this will likely be the last book I'll read by Barbara Michaels. The writing is fine and the book started out well, but it didn't hold my interest. Only sheer doggedness took me to the last page.

Other Worlds consists of two novellas, *The First Evening* and *The Second Evening*. The evenings are connected by what is most intriguing about the book. A group of turn of century personalities, including Houdini, Arthur Conan Doyle, Frank Podmore, and Nandor Fodor—this is the turn of the nineteenth century—gather in the astral world to discuss two cases of poltergeist activity. Everyone knows who the first two personalities are. Only a person stuffed like I am with useless knowledge recognizes who the latter two are.

The first evening of their discussion concerns the poltergeist that haunted the Bell family in early nineteenth century Tennessee. I've been told by people who claim to know that this is a famous case in parapsychological circles. The second case concerns the poltergeist that haunted the family of Reverend Phelps in nineteenth century Connecticut. I do not know if the Phelps's case is famous.

The structure of the book is appealing. These famous personalities, all of whom dabbled in spiritualism in one way or another, intend to sort out and explain events. (Andrew Jackson Davis, the "Seer of Poughkeepsie" and a precursor of Edgar Cayce, the Psychic Sage of Virginia Beach, appears as a character in the Phelps case.) The explanations fall along predictable lines. Houdini suggests fraud, Conan Doyle claims it's the real thing, and Podmore and Fodor offer psychological explanations of various complexity. No resolution is achieved and no explanation is rendered as final. Readers are given leave to decide for themselves whether the hauntings are legitimate or not.

The astral arguments among the four gentlemen take up only a fraction of the text. The bulk of the book describes the Bell and Phelps hauntings in excruciating detail. The Bell haunting starts out creepy enough. Black shapes are seen in the forest, doors open and close of their own accord, God-fearing country folk fall ill for no obvious reason. Ectoplasm soon thickens into molasses. There are only so many pranks a poltergeist can pull and, overall, the violence is tame. And there are only so many reactions possible among the characters—overall, the personalities of the afflicted families are bland. The first dish that spins off the dining room table headed for a character's forehead is scary; the tenth dish elicits a yawn. The first knife that propels itself across the room on the way to a character's throat is terrifying; the tenth knife doesn't cause so much as a visual blench.

The Phelps case is less interesting than the Bell case and that case ceases to be of interest after page fifty. At page one hundred there's a feeling of déjà vu. At page one hundred fifty there's real doubt as to the intention of the author.

At page two hundred there's a feeling that you are slipping, agonizingly slowly, into a small pit-trance. Maybe Michaels could have jazzed up the cases. This is fiction, after all, or a fictionalized account. We needn't summon Steven Spielberg for verbal special effects. As rendered in deadening detail the book summons The Sandman, and that's a shame, given the promising start.

FOUND AGAIN IN PENSACOLA

Pensacola—May, 2003

May 4

Babci and I left Little Egg Harbor at 5:30 AM. We arrived at Newark Airport around 7:30. The ride north was uneventful. There was only one wrong turn at the airport. A quick comment by Babci inspired me to swing into valet parking rather than into the long-term lot. No damage was done, we were not delayed, and we saved $28.00 a day.

After we checked in at the ticket counter—painlessly at eight o'clock on a Sunday morning—I went to the men's room and Babci stayed in the food court. She bought two coffees, placed them on a table, and turned around to do or get something. When she turned back, the coffees were gone. This vexed Babci mightily, since she thought someone stole them. I thought a cleaning lady took them—a person would have to be pathetic to steal someone's coffee in this era of contagious diseases. A number of this class prowl the food court, hastily dumping what they believe to be garbage into little carts they wheel from table to table. Babci was right to be annoyed, since she paid more than three dollars for the coffees, and I wondered what else the cleaning ladies swipe off the tables and drop in those little carts.

It was an auspicious start—two wrong turns and we weren't off the ground—but the ride to Pensacola went without incident. The first leg of the trip—on a Northwest Airlines plane leaving Newark at 9:55 AM and arriving at 11:46 in Memphis, the self-entitled "Distribution Center of America"—was the easiest domestic flight I ever had. The seats were wide and the plane was half empty. The second leg of the trip was more typical of flying. This was a crowded Pinnacle Airlines plane leaving Memphis at 12:55 PM and arriving in Pensacola at 2:14. Pinnacle, which is a subsidiary of Northwest, must hire comedians for flight attendants. Our attendant was a heavyset black man who cracked jokes as he rehearsed the safety drill. A heavyset flight attendant of the white complexion also cracked jokes during the safety drill on our 2001 visit. Probably, they were the same jokes.

I pay attention, but I've always thought these safety drills are on the useless side. Deep down, do we really believe we can use seat cushions as flotation devices in the event we ditch in the Atlantic? As it is, we weren't even flying over water, except for a few rivers and bayous here and yonder. Maybe the attendants should have left this part of the drill out and tried traditional stand up instead.

For the record, our return flight was on a Pinnacle plane leaving Pensacola at 10:40 AM Friday, May 9, and arriving in Memphis at 12:04 PM. The flight attendants on the return flight were buff and told no jokes during the safety drill. We left Memphis on a Northwest flight at 12:55 PM and arrived in Newark at 4:34. Little Egg Harbor was two rush hours to the south.

Jason, Ginny, Shane, and Evan met us in the airport. Jason was heavier than when we saw him last. He says he weighs 210 pounds, all of it muscle. This is more than I weigh—two hundred pounds, all of it—a-hem—muscle. Ginny looked slimmer than last time—I think it has to do with the fact that she is not in a motherly way this visit. She had a reddish tint to her hair and a healthy tan. I recall her saying something about going to a tanning salon. I think I remembered this because I thought it odd that someone who lives in the Sunshine State would go to a salon to get tan.

The boys looked handsome, dressed in matching clothing. The blond hair and wholesome complexions come gratis from God and Gregor Mendel. Shane is now four years old. He's a lanky little guy with a lot of athletic interest and capability. He's somewhat angular and definitely resembles Ginny more than Jason. Evan, who we referred to as "Evan, poo poo diaper baby," is less than two years. This makes him softer, rounder, and less competent. He's still a baby really, but he tries to do everything his *big brother* does, oh, does he try.

I dusted off my old jokes about buying Shane and Evan and taking them back to New Jersey. Five hundred dollars is the going rate, $750 for both boys. I teased Shane about him coming home with us and about having a nonstop party in New Jersey. Ice cream and snacks and cookies and cakes and lots and lots of fun, all day long and all week long. He can play baseball and soccer till his heart's desire. And he doesn't have to go to school. He can stay home all day and play. To my surprise, he didn't take the offer. I suppose he's a bit young to get the joke.

Shane is a real talkaholic—like all four year olds, he is highly opinionated. He has a definite Southern accent and talks with a certain twang. Evan doesn't say much. He just walks around, tries to climb things, looks at you, and smiles. Occasionally, he lets out a yell or a peal of laughter. And he cries, but not too often. I don't recall a single sustained crying episode. He must be too busy to cry.

The original plan was for Babci and me to ride in the Yorks' van. As the saying goes, "The best made vans—." In the interim they traded in the gray van they had in 2001 for a yellow pickup truck. This truck, although gigantic, holds a limited number of people and we preferred not to ride with the sheep in the back. So, we used a rental for the trip. I don't recall the make, but it was the right size and got us where we wanted to go, which was to quite a number of places, as it turned out.

I remarked on the drive to the motel that I had seen souvenirs in the Memphis Airport for a football team called *Volunteers*, a name I thought astoundingly bad for a major college franchise. *Volunteers* just doesn't do it in a section where football is second only to Jesus and Him crucified. *Volunteers* is a word that doesn't strike fear into the hearts of opponents; rather, it strikes wonderment in the minds of people who encounter it on trinkets in gift shops in airports. *Volunteers?* Why not *Recruits* or *Consultants* or *Part-time Temporaries?* Why not *Emergency Room Technicians* or *Respiratory Therapists* or *Phlebotomists?* Or to mention my own occupations, why not *Inventory Planners* or *Adjunct Professors?* Any of these titles would inspire as much fear and be as informative as the unsalted word *Volunteers.*

Jason informed us that the big news in the Panhandle was that a local football coach had recently resigned after running up an astronomical tab consorting with loose women he—a-hem—met after practice in a gentleman's club. The party he paid for concluded in a hotel room where the coach proceeded to let off pent-up competitive steam to the tune of thousands of the booster club's donations. To everyone's amazement, the ladies didn't *volunteer* to perform their patriotic duty gratis, not even for a head coach of football.

95

When we arrived at the Yorks' residence—2328A Smith Ave., an address I know well, having mailed probably a hundred letters there—we wanted to talk and to play with the boys. Shane was set to go. He kicked his sneakers off and we promptly located a hole in his sock. Babci said he had a "jura", which is phonetic Polish for "hole". Shane wanted to know what a *jura* is. Babci told him. Later, he kept referring to the hole in his sock as a "jura hole", which is redundant, except that Shane was unknowingly talking in two languages. This is a marvelous example of cultural transmission, which sets us apart as a species from the great apes, along with our higher intelligence and better looks. Babci heard "jura" from her parents, who got it from their parents, and so on, meandering through the centuries from the Wilenska district of Southeastern Lithuania to Escambia County, Florida.

Later, I played "piggies" with Shane, giving each tiny toe a separate destination. "This toe goes to the market, this toe goes to the golf course, this toe goes to the beach, this toe goes to church, this toe goes to the toy store." And then onto the other five piggies. And then back to the first five, and so on round and round till I ran out of destinations.

2328A Smith Ave. is in a community for military families. It is a gated community, with a MP at the gate. The first visit requires that you log in your destination, license plate, and driver's license. On subsequent visits you have to inform the officer on duty that you're on the log. The system worked well, although I noticed different levels of efficiency. One MP, a muscular guy with a crew cut, was preoccupied on the phone ordering pizza with extra cheese and a liter bottle of soda. I like to think he was as efficient as he looked—he waved us on with a dynamic flourish—but then we weren't wearing turbans or singing Allah's praises as we crossed the checkpoint.

To this day I've never learned who the *Smith* in 2328A Smith Avenue is. He has to be a military figure, but I'm not sure from which conflict. There was a Smith in the Korean War and there were a number of Smiths in the Civil War, notably "Baldy" Smith, who was a crony of Grant's and who led a brigade in the 1864 Virginia campaign. There must have been Smiths in World Wars One and Two, but I can't name one.

The community appeared somewhat congested and with plenty of children. Each house was one level, with a garage and grassy front lawn. The interior of the house is much larger than appears from the street. Entrance is into the living room. The bedrooms are to the right, along with a spacious bathroom. The living room is all of a piece with the kitchen, which leads to the garage. A counter divides the space into two rooms. There is a central block or work table in the middle of the kitchen. The computer station is across from the sink.

Babci and I stayed at the Comfort Inn at Three Warrington Road. This was the same place I stayed at when I visited Pensacola for the first time in June, 1994. Jason is currently the Navy's East Coast Teacher of the Year—an amazing achievement, considering he was never East Coast Pupil of the Year. In 1994 he was a lowly swabbie in rank. O.J. Simpson's infamous Bronco excursion along the Los Angeles freeways occurred the first night of my visit. Jason and I watched the chase and subsequent events at the mansion where O.J. was taken into custody.

I remember exactly where I was when I heard the news that the jury found O.J. not guilty. I was with Babci at the Mormon Family History Library in New York City the afternoon of October 3, 1995. The Mormon missionaries made no secret of their disappointment at the verdict. They were white people from Utah and had judged O.J. on the basis of his skin color. Surely, a black jury would never do such a thing.

May 5

Today was the day for Perdido Key, a place I wanted to visit since my first trip to Pensacola. For some reason I had been led to believe that Perdido Key was an uninhabited wonderland. I found out it's a wonderland, but not uninhabited. I suppose I should have heeded Oscar Wilde's witticism to the effect that the only thing worse than not visiting a place you want to visit is visiting it.

After a breakfast of coffee, bagels, and mini-muffins, Babci and I drove to Smith Ave. I'm proud to say we did not get lost. For honesty's sake I should clarify this and write that Babci got up before I did, walked to the dining room behind the pool, had the complimentary breakfast there, and returned to the room with my coffee, bagel, and mini-muffin. Being human, I know this is what is referred to as "the good life".

We found out when we arrived at 2328A Smith Ave. that Jason had to report to duty, despite the fact that he was on vacation. Another war hadn't broken out. Something more important had happened. A high muck-a-muck from Washington, DC, was going to visit the base the following day and the staff had to rehearse their greeting. (We never rehearsed in Barnes & Noble when executives visited.) It turns out this guy never showed up, which was good for us or Jason would have missed a second day.

There was a little more confusion since Jason had taken the big yellow truck to the base and the car seats for the boys happened to be in it. Ginny and I had to drive to the base and retrieve the seats. I got to see the building where Jason teaches. It's a monster of a place, the second longest building in the world. (The Pentagon is the longest.) The grounds resemble a college more than a military base.

An array of parking lots lies in front of a number of obviously academic buildings. Faculty and administrators get to park closer than the students, which is only fair. As Teacher of the Year Jason gets a spot near the front door. That made the truck easy to locate. Given its brilliant exterior, the truck wouldn't have been difficult to locate if it were in the remote section of the lot where the dunces park.

Before we left for the beach I filmed Babci and the boys. She's a little weaker and warier than the last time she played with them, but Babci still has *the touch* with children. Patience, kindness, and fun—that's what Babci offered Jason twenty years earlier and that's what she offered Shane and Evan. She played the same games and engaged in the same word play. Shane ate the attention up—he didn't care how long I filmed, so long as someone played with him. Little did he know that he was playing with the *A Number One Babci* in America—we can throw in Lithuania as well. For his part Evan strolled from chair-to-chair and smiled. He didn't have a clue what was going on and it didn't bother him.

The geography of this part of Florida resembles the lower Jersey Shore. It consists of a series of barrier islands that separate the mainland from the ocean. These islands, which are mostly long and slender, can be thought of as a series of pencils that lie on a saltwater blotter. The longer pencils are nearest the ocean. The stubs are closer to the mainland. Shavings serve for salt marshes, and there are plenty of them. The pencils lie end-to-end, but the ends never touch—in actuality, the gaps are channels and inlets. At the end of each pencil lies a fort. Fort Pickens is at the western tip of Pensacola Beach. Across the inlet is the place on Perdido Beach where Fort McRee used to stand. (Fort McRee consists of underwater ruins. The ruins can be visited by scuba diving, which leaves me out.) Some fifteen or more miles to the west on Perdido Key lies Fort Morgan, which we did not visit. Across the width of Mobile Bay lies Fort Gaines, which we visited later in the week. I suppose you can skip from ruined fort-to-fort along these barrier islands until you fall off the edge of the free world.

Access to Perdido Key is along Gulf Beach Highway, which crosses the intercoastal waterway on a simple truss bridge. Unlike the bridges on Jersey roads, there are no tolls, but then this isn't much of a bridge. And it's not much of a waterway at this point either.

I had expected Perdido Key to be a wilderness of sand and surf, and so it is. It is also an unbroken wall of hotels, motels, summer homes, condominiums, upscale gated communities, gift shops, and strip malls. Most of the architecture is pretty bad—not for anything is this stretch called the *Redneck Riviera*. The largest building and architecturally the worst I remember is "The Eden". This monster vaguely resembles a bivalve mollusk, which I hope was the intention of the architect. The towers extend in serrated fashion from a small central hub. The color of the complex is silvery white. The overall impression of the towers is tinny. Tacky, I should say.

Altogether, Pensacola Beach appeared more wild and natural. And the architecture was on a smaller size. Not better, but smaller, which is to its credit. I tend to think that the uncontaminated glories of nature that exist on Perdido Key lie on Johnson Beach, which we didn't visit. Johnson Beach is on the easternmost end of Perdido Key. It extends from the bridge all the way to where Fort McRee used to stand. Much of it is inaccessible by car, which left us out.

We pulled in a lot adjacent to the Gulf and visited the beach. Shane and I made it farthest, Babci about halfway, and Ginny not at all, since she had to tend to Evan, who was asleep. The highlight of our ramble on the beach was finding a dead skate. I thought it was a sting ray, but Luke told us differently when he saw the photographs and he knows about such things. The skate must have come ashore just before we arrived, as it was fresh and rather ferocious looking, despite being dead. Shane wasn't the least bit scared of its odd shape or of the fact that it had gone to the big fish house in the sky. He touched it and held it by the tail, which was quite tough despite its slender appearance, and pulled it a good ways along the beach, as he wanted to show his mother what we found. The skate was too heavy for Shane to pull for any distance and he abandoned it after about twenty yards. I wasn't about to pick it up or drag it—it was dead, after all. Ginny did come down later and view it, as did a few tourists who paused, bent over to take a look, and wisely kept on going. They weren't about to touch it either.

The beach we visited was a fairly rugged place. It was about a third the width of Wildwood. As might be expected on the Gulf, the sand was very white. After a little indecision about the legality—every sacred grain is rumored to be counted—I packed an empty soda bottle full of this white sand, brought it back to New Jersey, and made a nice decoration for the windowsill. The ocean was rough and unsettled. In this unprotected place, the ocean compared unfavorably with the green waters of Pensacola Beach. There were no life guards and no one was swimming. Except for the tourists, the few people on the beach were taking the sun from the hollowed gravities of their lounge chairs.

Some of the ruggedness might have been attributable to the awful humidity and to the oppressive glare. The ocean was soupy gray, the sand was stinging white, and the atmosphere was relucent with heat. Everything had a shimmering quality, and we have the pictures to show how fistic the light was. It was like looking through tin foil.

The only other specimens Shane and I found on our brief trek were ubiquitous mollusk shells lying on the beach. These shells, which are called *coquina*, are thickly grooved. Most are dark gray, although I found a large broken one that was bright orange. I immediately packed this one for the windowsill.

We didn't stay on the beach long, probably for no more than half an hour. We drove to an overpriced gift store and then to the place where, through the convenience of cell phones, Ginny arranged to meet Jason. When he joined us, we drove along the main drag—the only drag—and entered Alabama without fanfare, drum roll, or paperwork. The guidebook informed us that there is a popular bar at the Fla-bama border. This bar sponsors a contest in which participants throw mullets for distance. The winner gets a sack of mullet, along with public recognition for this particular talent. I shouldn't criticize this as a redneck activity, since some years ago the nation feverishly engaged in throwing midgets. I'm not sure what you got for winning that kind of contest. Maybe a little person in a sack.

We crossed back to the mainland over a small bridge and proceeded to a park in, or near, the city of Foley, Alabama. This park is an alligator preserve, but the most dangerous part of our visit was crossing a four-lane street to get to it.

The park consisted of an elevated walkway that led in crooked fashion over swampy ground. The water below was black and heavily overgrown with grass and reeds. There were signs warning about the dangers of alligators, as if we had to be reminded. Unfortunately, we didn't get to see any. In fact, we didn't see any life in the water. Jason pointed out the smeared grass on the muddy edges of the water where the alligators emerge to sleep after the tourists return to their comfy inns and before the evil teenagers come out.

From the park we drove to Lambert's, a famous Foley restaurant. The place is noted for the huge portions and for the odd behavior of the staff who stroll around and load up one's plate for the asking with all kinds of side dishes—potatoes, grits, okra, and salads. These side dishes are *in addition* to the immense meals that can be ordered off the menu a la carte. The staff is famous for throwing bread—no mullets or midgets. On request they will lob a roll across an aisle. If you look halfway athletic—this leaves me out—they will toss a roll across the room. I don't know what it is, but the people in these parts have a penchant for throwing things.

May 6

The day started with Babci's miraculous balancing act, bringing me another morning round of coffee, bagels, and mini-muffins, followed in a half hour by my walk for a refill of the reanimating *kavos*.

Jason and I drove Shane to preschool. I took a few pictures of Shane standing by the door of the school holding his knapsack. I was reminded of Jason as a preschooler. At that time Felicia lived in Hoboken and Jason attended day care in the church at Ninth and Clinton Sts. across from Hoboken High School. (This is my old "stomping ground", as Grandpa used to say—and it was Grandpa's old stomping ground, too. A different kind of stomping.) One afternoon I had to pick Jason up early. I entered and found the children lying on little cots, asleep supposedly. Of course, they were all pretending to be asleep, lying still with their eyes wide open.

And I remembered when Jason attended kindergarten in Our Lady of Grace School. One day he insisted on being a "big boy" and walking to school by himself. This meant a one-block tramp across Church Square Park in Hoboken. No big deal, geographically. But psychologically it was a big deal in little Jason's mind. And it was a big deal in my grown-up mind, since I was responsible for him. I could never have lived with myself if he went missing on my watch. After a good deal of crying and haggling—crying on his part, haggling on mine—I let him walk to school by himself—or so he thought. I followed a half-block behind. He never knew this at the time. Maybe he never knew this. It may be I'm letting a memory out of the knapsack for the first time.

Babci, Jason, and I drove downtown into the upscale heart of Pensacola to the Civil War Museum we missed visiting two years ago. This part of Pensacola, which is close to the water, resembles Hackensack in New Jersey. It's a mixture of courthouses, county offices, and family-operated stores and boutiques. Most of the buildings are old, ponderous, and one or two stories in height. The store fronts are old-fashioned, with lots of brickwork and with display windows on both sides of entrances set back from the street.

The museum kept Southern hours and opened at ten rather than at nine, so we were an hour early. We walked a few blocks to a park, where we sat and chatted until we were overcome by the cruel humidity. We took refuge in a sandwich shop for coffee, cookies, and additional chatting under the civilized invention of air conditioning.

When we left him Shane was the picture of life, opportunity, and futurity; I'm sure he was a little rumpled when Ginny picked him up at the close of school. The museum opened to images of suffering, death, and the dead past. Founded by Dr. Norman Haines Jr., it concentrates on the medical aspects of the Civil War. The medical implements on display are gruesome; some are downright grotesque. The Civil War was a century and a half ago, but these implements looked like something out of the Middle Ages. What was worse, they looked like something out of a *Hellraiser* movie. It makes you squeamish to see them—the *tools* of the medical profession in those days were heavier, larger, and cruder than our current medical instruments. You get more squeamish when you consider there was no anesthesia other than alcohol and primitive morphine. The squeamishness increases—by this time it's bubbling at throat level—when you recall there were lax standards of cleanliness. Surgeons *operated* without wearing gloves, washing their hands, changing clothes, sterilizing instruments, or taking the cigars out of their mouths.

There were more than six hundred thousand casualties in the Civil War. It is the second greatest catastrophe ever to descend on the United States—the first is the influenza epidemics of 1917 and 1918 in which approximately the same number ingloriously succumbed to *The Spanish Lady*. I don't have the statistics at hand, and I'm not sure they exist for the Confederacy, but a sizeable number of deaths can be attributed to disease and infection brought about by the lack of medical treatment. Another sizeable number of deaths can be attributed to the medical treatment available at the time. And I'm excluding from consideration the vast numbers of cripples, morphine addicts, and soldiers left psychologically disturbed by the war.

Dr. Haines has collected more than medical curiosities, which is refreshing else the exhibits become unbearably depressing. There's an impressive collection of antiques, collectables, relics, and autographs on display. A small room in the rear focuses on Civil War events in the vicinity of Pensacola. This room has on display the first Confederate national flag. This flag has eight stars irregularly arranged and two horizontal red stripes on either side of a central white stripe. The flag has an eventful history. It was captured by the Sixth New York in the battle near Fort Pickens on October 9, 1861. For many years the flag was kept on display in New York City and then in a private collection. Dr. Haines purchased it in 1994.

The lady who took our money at the door turned out to be an interesting person. She was middle-aged, with black hair and a distinctive accent I took for Pennsylvanian. (I soon found out she was from West Virginia, which is close enough.) I mentioned that I'm interested in local history on a small scale, such as the Pulaski massacre in Little Egg Harbor. And I mentioned that I was in favor of communities preserving and popularizing their local histories. I said that I had recently seen an article in our local paper how a community in West Virginia was divided over plans to open a museum and theme park on the Hatfield-McCoy feud. Some of the locals favored it as a way to raise funds and attract tourist dollars. Other locals opposed it because it glorified violence and made the community look bad, as if the West Virginia backwoods could be made to look bad by a handful of murders.

This lady grew excited at the news, since she was descended from one of the McCoys who didn't get plugged. I got an immense charge out of the coincidence that, in the first place, I should have noticed the article in *The Press of Atlantic City*, in the second place, mention the article to a guide in a Civil War museum in Pensacola and, in the third place, have the guide be related by blood to the feud. I was tempted to ask for an autograph. It wouldn't have been difficult to get, since the lady chased after me as I toured the exhibits and inquired several times about just when I saw the article and how she could get a copy. If I had known I'd meet a real McCoy, I'd have paid more attention at the breakfast table.

I purchased a nice portrait of Lt. General Richard Ewell in the bookstore of the museum. As I paid the lady mentioned that this was the first Ewell portrait sold in a year. Lee and Jackson sell much better, it goes without saying, and she said it. I commented that I was disappointed *Old Bald Head* sold so poorly, since I was recording secretary of the Richard Ewell Fan Club. The lady didn't bat an eye at my title and I'm sure she didn't think it was a fib. I don't look like the fibbing kind and she was too preoccupied with her ancestry to pay attention to anything I said. I was tempted to add, "Oh, by the way, I forgot to mention that great-granddad on the maternal side was a Hatfield," but I thought better than to joke about a feud. She might have kept a fully-loaded six-shooter under the counter, hidden beneath the Confederate tie clasps and nail clippers.

For what is likely to be the last time we visited McGuire's Irish Pub on Route 98. We arrived in the late afternoon so that the boys—meaning Shane—wouldn't act up. As I recall, everything worked out fine. I made a note that I had a vegetable platter. I don't remember the particulars, but it must have been a healthy portion. Or, as they say in these parts, *I reckon* it must have been a healthy portion. In McGuire's all portions are healthy, including the healthy ones.

McGuire's is famous for the dollars hanging from the walls. (The bills are markered with large black stripes, so they can't be used as tips.) The bills now number more than a hundred thousand dollars—a few dollars less if Shane had his way. But Shane's arms were too short to grab any dollars or to box with Daddy. I regret I didn't contribute to the thickening green thatch.

Around five o'clock we visited Big Lagoon State Park. This park is located on the southern tip of Pensacola, across from Perdido Key. The Big Lagoon refers to the intercoastal waterway that separates the mainland from Perdido. There's another body of water in the park. This one loops inland and is called The Grand Lagoon, although it doesn't seem as *grand* as the *big* lagoon. They must have different standards of measurement south of Mason-Dixon.

We walked to the water's edge at the Big Lagoon, stopping for a few minutes at a nearby playground, where we took turns pushing the boys on the swings. There were a number of picnic tables and grills in the area, but the park was empty at the late weekday hour.

It turned out the park wasn't as empty as I thought. As I wandered along the edge of the lagoon looking for a good spot to capture scenic pictures, a huge bird came swooping out of the trees unexpectedly. This bird, which stayed at the tree line, squawked and hooted and howled and barked, flapping its wings menacingly. I have to admit I was startled, nearly out of my pants and sneakers. For a moment I thought I had met the Mothman.

Jason said I probably wandered too near the bird's nest. This explanation made sense from the human perspective, but not from the avian. I would have to be twenty feet tall or be able to levitate to get at the nest, and there were plenty of picnic tables in the vicinity. During weekends and holidays this poor bird must be in a state of permanent rufflement.

Jason led us on a short hike that meandered along sandy soil from the parking lot to a walkway over a picturesque fishing pond. I can't say whether this pond was part of the Grand Lagoon or whether it was a separate enclosed body of water. The map isn't clear on this point. Whatever the geography, the place was scenic and tranquil. The black water was still and surrounded by lush green banks. In the late afternoon light the pond was a kind of mirror, which was the effect I tried, but failed, to capture on film—just like my eyes, my old camera doesn't capture detail anymore. I did get some nice pictures of the Yorks, including one of Jason and Shane that's on the shelf of my computer stand. I'm looking at it now, which is why I'm making a lot of typing mistakes.

Jason used pieces of bread as bait, but he and Shane didn't catch anything. A flotilla of beady reptilian periscopes quickly gathered as the bread disintegrated. I took these eyes as belonging to alligators—tiny ones, but alligators, nevertheless. It soon became obvious they belonged not to alligators but to turtles. Probably, they belonged to a vicious snapping breed.

The park advertises itself as the *real Florida*, and I believe it is. The vegetation is thick and green. There's hardly any soil showing through. There's no beach, as the plants grow right to the water's edge. As Jason fished I took a stroll in the woods. I followed a footpath that led around the pond for a while, but gave up when the insects started to come out. I was also worried about poisonous snakes darting from the tall grass and about the notorious Florida panther, a creature on the verge of extinction and not amused at its fate. I was also worried about those snapping turtles ambushing me and taking bites out of my heels. I'm very fond of my heels and wouldn't want to lose one; you might say I'm attached to them.

Our last stop in the park was an observation tower located near the water. To get to the tower we crossed a small bridge that spanned a marshy inlet over the Grand Lagoon. There were a number of old folks fishing on the bridge, but "fishing" is not the right word for what these people were doing. Their practice was to throw long nets into the water, which they then slowly retrieved. (One old guy skittered while standing in the water.) Technically, this is called seining—it can be done without hand gestures. They caught tiny black fish the size of sardines. I wasn't impressed, but they seemed to be happy, and Shane had a ball as they let him peel the fish from the nets and drop them in buckets.

A beautiful white bird stood poised in the marshes below the bridge. I don't know the species, but it must have been a crane or a swan. Unlike the savage creature that was on the verge of attacking me, this handsome bird was standing perfectly still. Probably, it was looking for tourists to film it.

The tower is a three or four story wood structure. Climbing to the top provides a *grand*—not *big*—view of the water looking to the south. The lagoon widens at this point. There's a small antler-shaped island just off shore. In the dusk the island serves as a steppingstone to the black porch of Perdido Key. Everything was profoundly serene. It was about this time that my camera ran out of film, which was fine, since the land was fast running out of light.

May 7

Today we drove to Biloxi, Mississippi. The drive was to the west on I-10, then to the south on Route 90. In Biloxi we passed a number of tall buildings just off the Interstate. Some of the buildings were industrial, others were office towers, nine were casinos. One casino is shaped like a pirate's ship. I'm sure the ship does a fine business, but I don't think I'd want to gamble in a *pirate's* ship, of all seaworthy vessels. The gaming business in these parts commenced in 1992. To assuage Evangelical souls, the casinos have to be on the Gulf shore.

The last portion of the trip ran directly along the Gulf. A beach of modest size paralleled the road. There were a number of palm trees on the beach; the trees are picturesque, but provide no shade. And there were a number of long thin walkways that extended over the water like miniature piers; these walkways concluded in small summerhouses. Every so often, tents and small huts arose on the sand selling beach chairs, umbrellas, and jet ski rentals. Sales must be poor, since the beach was mostly deserted. The day was brutally hot, humid, and overcast. Mississippi folk must have plenty of experience with this kind of weather and the sense to stay indoors—the stereotype is that they sit on rocking chairs on porches fanning themselves, drinking mint juleps, and speaking in euphemisms about family scandals.

Everything looked rather peaceful, baking in the white hot and horizonless glare. The Gulf was still and without any disturbances. There didn't seem to be any waves or no more than could be found on a large lake. Jason explained that the Gulf of Mexico is not as deep as the Atlantic, so it doesn't produce the same pattern of cresting waves. This sounds correct, although I have a sense that appearances can be deceiving—and that deceptions can be appearing. The Web site for Biloxi says the city has been devastated five times by hurricanes and I don't doubt that, considering how close everything is to the sea.

Like Pensacola, Biloxi has a rich and complex history. The earliest inhabitants can be traced to a few thousand years before Christ—this would have to be the Mormon Christ, since we are in the Western Hemisphere. Native American culture peaked in Biloxi in the sixteenth century, not so long before the coming of the Europeans, which meant, of course, the immediate collapse of Native American culture.

The first Europeans in Biloxi were French explorers who came ashore in 1699. The French had cordial relations with the Natives—the name of the tribe was *Biloxi*, which is logical enough. The French retained control until 1763, when they ceded the land to the British. Fortunately for the Biloxi, English rule lasted only thirteen years, when Spain took over. The Spanish influence ended in 1817, when the United States took over and Mississippi became a state.

Since its inception Biloxi has been a resort for wealthy Southerners. This is a tradition that lives on with the casinos. Residents fought for the Confederacy, but the town itself was in Union hands throughout the Civil War. After the Civil War Biloxi and its surroundings became the headquarters of seafood canneries in the United States. By 1910 it was the largest producer of oysters in America. I don't know if it retains this distinction.

The Biloxi Lighthouse is heavily advertised on the city's Web site, but it is not impressive. It's sixty-one feet tall, which is less than half the height of the lighthouse in Pensacola or of "Old Barney" on Long Beach Island in New Jersey. It stands on a median on Route 90 at Porter Ave. To access it, you have to cross a busy road, but this is an exercise in pointlessness, since the lighthouse is closed to the public. I took pictures from a beachfront parking lot. The main difficulty was locating an angle that included as much of the lighthouse and as little of telephone wires and traffic poles as possible.

The lighthouse dates from 1848. For much of its life it was tended by civilians, including by a lady named Maria Younghans, who kept the light for fifty three years. The Coast Guard took over in 1939. The light went out in 1968.

We visited Jefferson Davis's last home and presidential library, an estate called *Beauvoir* located a few miles west of the lighthouse on Route 90. I thought we would be the only visitors, but there were the requisite Confederacy admirers strolling about, mostly middle-aged white guys dressed in shorts, work shoes, and baseball caps. There were also several ladies who looked old enough to have socialized with Jeff and Varina. A gang of high schoolers entered the theater where we waited to watch a documentary on the life of Davis. (The wait greatly annoyed Babci, who had been led to believe the film would come on without delay—she mustn't like sitting in an air-conditioned theater looking at a blank screen.) I thought it was impressive that students visited a historical site rather than make the usual trip to a beach or to an amusement park at the close of the school year. Watching them troop in, I suddenly realized that all the students were Caucasian. There wasn't a single student of color among them. "This is odd," I thought, "There are no black high school students in Mississippi? That can't be." Of course, it can't be, but we were in Beauvoir, after all, home of the first and only president of the Confederate States of America.

There is little mention of slavery at Beauvoir. The short film we finally got to watch described how the war was fought over States' Rights rather than over slavery. The narrator described how in that time period Americans viewed themselves as belonging to particular states first and to a nation of *united states* second. This is true enough, but it is certainly not sufficient to describe the causes of that immense conflict. It would be like describing World War Two without referring to nationalism or to anti-Semitism.

The film described the warmth and personal loyalty of Jefferson Davis. The real-life Northern Congressman who served as the narrator had run up serious debts and had occasion to petition his friend to bail him out. Princely though the sum was, Davis immediately wrote a check and refused to charge interest on the loan. "Sirrh, there is never interest charged among friends," Davis reputedly insisted. I don't know if this story is true, but it goes a long way in revealing why Jefferson Davis, of all Secesh politicians, became the first and only president of the Confederate States.

We didn't get to see much of the library after the film. We toured a small museum devoted to Davis and then followed the tour markers around Beauvoir. The estate is not large and can be visited in an hour or two. The crushing heat made it feel as if the tour lasted four or five hours. I'm proud to say Babci accompanied us every step of the way—she must like walking in ninety degree temperature.

The great house where Jeff and Varina lived for the last ten years of his life is a typical Southern mansion of the period. Living quarters were on the upper two stories. The ground floor is really a decorative defense against flooding, which is imminently possible. The Gulf is literally across the street. We took some pictures of Babci standing by the gates of the property. I tried to match these up with the pictures we took some years ago behind St. Anne's Church in Vilnius, but they didn't come out as clear. The day had that all-white glare that is not conducive to Kodak clarity. Earlier, we did get a nice pose of Babci standing beside a magnolia tree in a small garden outside the presidential library.

We missed the most recent tour of the great house and it was too hot to wait for the next. I took pictures of the house and climbed the steep stairs that led to the porch. As befits great old southern houses, there was a porch that ran nearly around the entire structure. Of course, there were rocking chairs on the porch and old folks rocking on them. If we were in Utah, these old folks would be Mormons. In this part of the world they were probably of the Baptist faith.

A peculiarity of the house was that the kitchen was located in an adjoining building to the rear. The pamphlet says the kitchen was outside in order to minimize the risk of fires. Servants—*slaves* before the war—brought the food inside in a culinary bucket brigade.

Jeff and Varina lived in Beauvoir in the years 1877-89. By that time some of the animosities inspired by the Civil War had started to die out, as did the animosity holders. Davis was among the longest lived of the leaders of the time, dying at eighty-one years of age. He became, if not a respected citizen, at least a recognizably historical one. Many people visited Beauvoir to meet and interview him. One of the least likely visitors was Oscar Wilde, the Irish fop and gay blade, who stopped on one of his speaking tours. This must have been one of the oddest Beauvoir dinner parties, considering Davis's stern reputation and Wilde's eccentric appearance and personality. But then, maybe it wasn't—Wilde was known as being handy with his fists in a brawl and Davis had attempted in 1865 to avoid capture dressed in a shawl.

After we toured the area around the library and great house we strolled up a short path toward the Tomb of the Confederate Unknown—but *strolled* isn't the right word. The path was flat, but the heat and palpable humidity made the walk feel like we were climbing a mountain. The Tomb is surprisingly unimpressive. It's a waist-high marble monument enclosed in a gate bordered by small American flags. No fanfare, no overstatement, no exaggeration, and no controversy. You wonder who's in the grave, and what field of battle he was retrieved from, and where he lived, and what his name was, and what kind of person he was. You wonder how old he was when he died. The Unknown was someone from somewhere. You remember there are a lot of Confederate unknowns.

Our age is very different. Every individual casualty is precious and everything that happens on any battlefield anywhere in the world is carried on the evening news for everyone to second guess. It wasn't like that in the 1860s. The families of Confederate Unknowns never found out the fates of their husbands and fathers and sons. Confederate battle reports and rosters were haphazardly prepared. Knowledge of events on the battlefield would have been by letter, by word of mouth, and by newspaper articles. No news was instantaneous. If they came, letters were long delayed. All the people at home knew is that their loved ones *just never came back.*

We left Biloxi and drove along Route 90, gradually heading inland. Our next stop was the Barnes & Noble in Gulfport. This was a decent-sized store located at the edge of a mall. Ginny bought some books for the kids, which was the intention of the visit. Babci complained about things until she stopped in the café and ordered a frappachino, after which she stopped complaining. A deliciously cool frappachino on an oppressively hot day will instantly convert a person to the joys of amicability.

There occurred an existential moment while Jason and I waited in the café. A deaf-mute lady came by, grunting and gesturing for us to sign a petition for a deaf-mute softball league. I'm not sure whether she was soliciting funds—this is not allowed in Barnes & Noble, and it says so on the door— but Jason gave her five dollars. She was so overjoyed, the grunting and the gesturing increased. She walked away excitedly—and left the petition on the table. The existential moment lies in this—how do you attract the attention of a deaf-mute going in the opposite direction? You can't call after her, "Hey, you forgot your petition!" You can't gesture with a wave of the hand, "Hey, come back here!" You can't do anything but sit and stare at one another and at the petition lying on the table and at the back of the lady receding in the reference aisle. It's one of *those moments.*

I'm happy to report the lady got her petition back, although I'm not sure how. Perhaps she remembered she was leaving without the most important piece of paper, although five dollars isn't bad. Maybe we caught the attention of a person in front of the lady who then turned her around. All I know is the situation was resolved, probably after a lot more grunting and gesturing.

May 8

Today we traveled to Fort Gaines, which is on Dauphin Island on the Alabama coast. The drive was along I-10 to Route 163, which runs southward alongside the bay in the little stump of Alabama that borders the Gulf. Actually, it's less a geographical stump than the leg of a seven-footer. The trip took a lot longer than anyone thought.

The initial portion of Route 163 off the interstate is through a suburb of Mobile. The area doesn't seem to be doing well economically, since there were a lot of closed shops and empty strip malls. The McDonald's we stopped in on the return trip was prospering, however. It had an air-conditioned playroom where Shane romped for half an hour.

Route 163 crosses desolate scenery for quite a distance—to continue the leg metaphor, this stretch is the shinbone. It's one way in each direction with a border of tangled maritime forest obscuring the destinations of dirt roads that lead to who knows where. Although there were a number of well-appointed homes on the bay side, most of the buildings were run down and ramshackle. Many had "For Sale" signs posted on the lawns.

The most southerly portion of Route 163 crosses over a few small bridges sheltering flotillas of powerboats—we're at the ankles now. A number of industries were visible in the distance, including a gargantuan power station and what appeared to be several strip mining operations.

We stopped for gas and for directions at a Chevron station somewhere on the way. The attendant was a small, stocky lady of copper complexion and startling gray eyes. I just knew looking at those eyes that she had occult abilities. If I'm lucky, she won't steal my soul and add it to the collection she keeps in bottles next to the chewing gum under the counter. She had lived for too long near *the other place* not to own powers of black witchcraft. (It could be she had lived too near the power station.) Fortunately, I was on the spiritual ball. I had no intention of spending eternity in a display case. When she made change for the gas, I borrowed a lyric from Bluesman Lindner and whispered, "Satan strong, but Jesus stronger." She didn't reply, although I heard a hiss under her breath.

We crossed to Dauphin Island over an impressive and highly scenic bridge. Most of the bridge ran only a few feet over Mobile Bay, which appeared shallow and brown. About halfway over, the bridge rose dramatically to allow large ships entrance into this portion of the waterway. Since everything else on the horizon was perfectly flat, the effect was unnerving—the highway was like a roller coaster as we zipped along at seventy miles an hour up and over the concrete hill. The view from the top is breathtaking—the white road drops toward the brown water at a steep angle. But you can't pay too much attention to the view. You have to pay more attention to the speedometer, else you arrive on Dauphin Island from the air.

Like many of the barrier islands on the Gulf coast, Dauphin Island has an interesting past, having been claimed by five nations—six, if you count Native Americans—across its complicated history. The first European to arrive was Alonzo Pineda in 1519. He didn't stay long. In 1699 a French explorer with the wonderful name of Pierre le Moye de'Iberville established a colony on what became Dauphin Island. Pierre named it *Massacre Island* because of the large burial ground found there. Tourism was not good. A few years later the name was changed to *Dauphin Island* after the heir to the French throne. Tourism improved.

Fort Gaines is an impressive site on the eastern tip of the island. The Gulf laps at the shore a short walk away. "Laps" is the correct word. As we observed in Biloxi, the water resembles a lake more than an ocean. The waves are gentle and barely noticeable. The beach is nonexistent. The wrack is a stone curb next to the parking lot. Fort Morgan, which lies across the bay, is visible in clear weather. Unfortunately, the day was intolerably humid and hazy, so we couldn't see it. We could hardly discern the array of oil derricks sitting offshore. Jason told us the oil derricks were causing political controversy. Some people have the idea that the United States should become oil independent from the Middle East and find alternative resources off our coasts. This is not a bad idea. Other people are worried that drilling so close to the heavily populated shoreline risks environmental disaster. This is not a moot concern.

The present fort was built by slave labor in the 1850s. The fort was named for Edmond Pendleton Gaines, a prominent soldier of the early nineteenth century, although unknown today. Gaines fought in the War of 1812, which is also unknown today, and participated in the capture of the renegade Vice President Aaron Burr. The fort, although militarily obsolete shortly after its construction, remained active into the 1950s, serving as a gunnery school and as a Coast Guard station.

Mobile Bay was the site of a major Civil War battle in August, 1864. At that time Mobile was one of the last ports available to Confederate blockade runners. These were private ships that risked boarding or worse to run the Union blockade and bring much needed foreign supplies to the strangled Confederacy. The Union intention that summer was to close the port in Mobile and suffocate the Confederacy.

A force of fifteen hundred Union troops landed west of Fort Gaines on August 4. A day later Admiral David Farragut took a fleet of four ironclads and fourteen wooden vessels into Mobile Bay. Forts Gaines and Morgan poured a devastating fire on the fleet. The ironclads were immune to the shelling, but they were endangered by a different type of martial innovation— mines, called *torpedoes* in those days. The monitor *Tecumseh* struck a torpedo and sank, taking ninety three sailors with it. The effect of the loss of the

Tecumseh was so disturbing, the fleet faltered, causing Farragut to utter the line which history remembers him for—"Damn the torpedoes! Full steam ahead!" History doesn't remember his other line that day—"Damn that Lincoln! This is another nice mess he's gotten me into."

Once past the range of the guns of Forts Gaines and Morgan, the fleet was inside the harbor and Mobile was lost to the Confederacy. A single rebel ironclad, the *Tennessee*, took up the fight, but it was a hopeless cause. The *Tennessee* shortly surrendered. Fort Gaines held out for two days before it surrendered.

If you consider the previous metaphor suggesting that barrier islands can be considered as pencils lying on a saltwater blotter, you can picture the forts as erasers on the ends of the pencils. There are Pickens and McRee in Pensacola Bay and Gaines and Morgan in Mobile Bay. You can also consider the fact any child—or anxious adult—knows. Erasers are easily bitten off. The battle of Mobile Bay demonstrated that the mammoth forts built on the American coastline in the first half of the nineteenth century were obsolete by the second half of the nineteenth century.

The use of stationary mines was a controversial moral issue in the 1860s—we've come a long way since. People in that age didn't mind killing with weapons that moved, but had qualms about using hidden or stationary weapons. The use of mines also demonstrated how rapidly technology had changed. In the days following the battle two ironclads and five wooden vessels sank in Mobile Bay after striking mines.

Fort Gaines is an imposing structure. It's the best preserved of the three forts we visited on our travels to the Gulf. It has five walls, each massive and grim and built of millions of aging bricks that are generally gray in complexion and mixed with hepatic splatters of red, dark green, and brown. At the corners of the walls are well-preserved bastions. Thirty-two-inch cannons stand on a few of the bastions. They are on concrete rails. Long wooden rudders allow for positioning. A range-finding station existed behind the east bastion. These cannons look as if they can throw shells into the next time zone.

The fort vaguely resembles home plate in outline. It looks toward an ocean of a playing field—some hot ones were served on that field in August, 1864. Oil derricks can serve as outfielders.

Entrance is across a dry moat and into a gift shop. A disagreeable lady took our money on the way in and advised us to watch our step. This was sensible advice, considering the height of the parapets and the steep ladders that led up and down. I stopped in the gift shop after our tour, but the lady at the register still looked so disagreeable I decided not to buy anything just to spite her. I whispered as I walked out, "Satan strong, but Jesus stronger." I'm pretty sure I heard a hiss.

There's an impressive relic in the parking lot. It's a huge remnant of a ship's keel that washed ashore during a storm some years ago. No one knows the name of the ship. Presumably, the rest of it lies on the floor of the Gulf. I tend to think the floor of the Gulf is a littered place.

The iron anchor of Admiral Farragut's flagship, the USS *Hartford*, sits at the center of the fort. From a distance the anchor resembles the skeleton of a car or truck; it looks the same close up. Farragut, who was an elderly officer and an old foggy (although no one called him that to his face), preferred to fight with wooden vessels rather than with ironclads. We know this is not forward-looking thinking, but the *Hartford* must have been quite the wooden vessel, considering the size of its anchor.

Here's one for the "It's a small world" department. I had heard of David Farragut, but I had never heard of the name of his flagship or I forgot it, if I had. Six weeks after we viewed the anchor of the *Hartford* in Fort Gaines, Babci and I viewed another relic in The Mariners' Museum in Newport News, Virginia. This was an immense wooden beam the length of a tractor trailer hanging from the ceiling in one of the museum's exhibit halls. The beam was from the keel of the *Hartford*. It was painted a bright color, possibly gold, and was slightly curved, like a bow. A very impressive piece. I don't know where the rest of the *Hartford* is or what became of her, but I have the feeling that if we make enough tours and visit enough forts and museums, we might get to reconstruct the ship in its entirety.

There are a few free-standing buildings inside the fort. To the immediate right of the gift shop lies a single-story building that was the officer's quarters. This building used to be three stories, but the top two were burned in the battle. The four hundred enlisted men stationed at Gaines slept in tents outside the fort.

A number of shops run alongside the interior walls. These include a blacksmith's shop and forge, a bakery, and a latrine. The latrine could accommodate twenty men at a sitting. The tide came up twice a day and took the refuse with it. Swimming was not recommended.

If you don't mind the stupefying humidity it's possible to tour the powder and ammunitions sheds tucked inside the walls. Although technically obsolete in the sense Gaines couldn't defeat the ironclads, the fort possessed a clever system of elevators and lifts to get the ammunition atop the bastions. At one point later in its history there was a gun that could be raised and lowered from inside a shed.

The upper deck or terreplein leads from bastion to bastion. It's possible to walk atop four of the five walls—the fifth is not intact. You have to be careful, since the path is uneven and the ground looks to be twenty feet distant. The terreplein, which is wider than what I remembered of Pickens or Barrancas, consists of two levels, one slightly higher than the other.

There is an indentation on the interior western wall. A placard informs us that the indentation was made by a shell from the USS *Chickasaw*. This is more than a little scary, considering that the shell crossed the entire interior portion of the fort to strike this spot. After hitting the wall, the shell would have fragmented and skipped in the reverse direction. I don't think it would have been deterred by human impediments. I like to think people were shorter in those days.

We didn't explore the rest of Dauphin Island, which meanders for fifteen or more miles to the west. The central span of the island looked to be all of two blocks wide. A single street ran in the middle. Sand was everywhere, sand on the main street, and sand on the side streets, such as they were. The sand was the whitest I ever saw—it looked more like snow than like sand. I was severely tempted to grab a jarful for the windowsill. The houses were large and elevated as a protection against storms, of which there must be a fair number. The houses also looked upscale and quite modern, as if they had been built recently. The place reminded me of Long Beach Island in New Jersey, although it was more rugged and desolate. We didn't see a single pedestrian or biker. There was hardly any traffic. I wonder if anyone lives here.

Everyone was getting cranky and hungry, so we cut the tour short. It seemed pointless to proceed, since we didn't know if there was a bridge leading back to the mainland from the western end of the island. The single eatery we passed was a mom-and-pop operation—no fast food and no children allowed. So, we drove like the dickens back to the McDonald's we spotted south of Mobile.

That evening, Babci, Jason, and I went to Shane's T-ball game, which I filmed. I should say I filmed Shane to the exclusion of the other players, all of whom were in the four-to-seven year range. Ginny stayed home with Evan, who is too young to join a league even in the precocial country of Florida. After the game we returned to 2328A Smith Ave. for the last time. Ginny cooked spaghetti as a farewell dinner.

Shane has a future ahead of him in baseball. The little guy really slammed the ball, including one shot straight up the middle. That kind of shot is a solid single in any league. Shane really put the wood to the ball, which is proof that the branch doesn't fall far from the tree.

Shane showed his age in the outfield, however. He fooled around most of the time with the *other* right fielder, a four-year-old named Cody. (Before the game, Cody complained to Jason that Shane punched him. Jason told Cody to punch him back. Except when Billy Martin was managing, this kind of thing doesn't happen in the Yankees' dugout.) Shane dropped to the ground and, rather than pay attention to what was happening at home plate, dug in the dirt and threw his glove and hat in the air. His hat toss wasn't too bad, considering that one of the left fielders threw his hat over the outfield fence.

At one point Shane ran off the field, to the consternation of the coaches. He kept on going, all the way at full speed around the dugout and to Jason. Coach Big Poppa, who was standing on the third-base side, yelled to the coach standing on the first-base side, "Where's Shane going?" I suppose Big Poppa must have thought Shane intended to keep going onto the street and out onto the highway and head north to Yankee Stadium. The first-base coach replied and everyone in the bleachers found out that an inning can last longer than a four-year-old's bladder.

In T-ball, an inning can last longer than a fifty-year-old's bladder.

Travel Talk

I asked Shane on one of our long drives whether his Grandma and Granddad smoke cigarettes. He said, "No." I asked whether his Mom smokes. He said, "No." I asked whether his Dad smokes. He said, "No, but he uses dip, just like Coach Big Poppa." Shane put a Southern twist on "dip", so it came out sounding like "dee-ip". Shane then went on to imitate Coach Big Poppa, using the strongest, most intense accent, "Heet that b-a-a-ll, son, heet that b-a-a-ll."

We had a lot of good conversations during our visit, but the quote of the trip belongs to Shane. During one of our long drives—I don't remember whether it was to or from Biloxi or Dauphin Island—Shane got reprimanded for doing something *bebber*, as Babci would say in colloquial Polish. After a few minutes of silence filled with serious mentation, Shane announced to the front seat in particular and to the future in general, "When I get to be a Daddy, just watch!"

I don't doubt it.

May 9

The last day of a visit with loved ones is always distressing, although it's not as distressing at the time as afterward. At the time you're worried about making the airline connections and getting home in reasonably good order. We had two planes to catch and, what can be as bad, we had to drive to Little Egg Harbor on the Garden State Parkway. And there was always the weather. The weather on the ground in Pensacola was fine, but there was the memory of that awful day we spent traveling home in June, 2001. Until we went through the metal detectors and got in the arcade, we never knew what the season would spring on Memphis or, further along, on Newark.

As it turned out, the trip home was uneventful and, remarkably, on time. Even the Garden State Parkway was kind to us. The only grief was taking leave of the Yorks.

During my first visit to Pensacola in the summer of 1994 Jason was unmarried and without children. When we visited in June, 2001, he was married with one son and a second on the way. And he had advanced in rank as well. When we visited in May, 2003, there were two sons and a still higher rank. And there was the "Teacher of the Year" honor, for which he got recognition and a parking space. I think Pensacola is a lucky place for them, but the Yorks can't wait to leave. Their next stop is Jacksonville, which will bring them a short drive from Ginny's parents. I think they will continue to prosper in Jacksonville. And I like to think there would have been additional children and a higher rank had I visited Pensacola for the fourth time.

Who can say how much Shane and Evan will have grown when we see them next? And I wonder how Ginny will be making do in her home city and how Jason's career in the service will be progressing. I think the next rank is *Chief.* For that matter, I wonder how the world situation will be. We seem to be in a basket and on our way, as the saying goes. But I don't feel so bad about things when I think of the fine family we left in Florida and of those two lovable rascals starting out in life.

Some people have Paris, but for me there will always be Pensacola, and memories of the blue green waters of the Gulf, and of the hundred thousand greenbacks hanging from the walls of McGuire's Irish Pub, and of the white sand of Pensacola Beach and the snow-white sand of Dauphin Island, and of Shane sitting in the low water in Santa Rosa Sound with five adults fussing over him, and of Matthew and Luke clowning in the somewhat deeper water, and of a slightly older Shane dressed in a green uniform and banging one through the middle, just like *his old man* (but not like his *great* uncle), and of Evan traipsing contentedly from couch to rocking chair and back to the couch, and of two exasperating car rides and of a kindly old lady in a gas station somewhere in town, and of fourteen people dressed in white ponchos strolling New Orleans in a tropical thunderstorm, and of rushing with Jennie through the creepy passages in the walls of Fort Barrancas, and of a private excursion to Fort Pickens where Babci climbed the battlements with a deft step and, two years later, of Babci, gimpy but still game, wandering Fort Gaines and the ferociously hot grounds of Beauvoir, and of seeing how Ginny is raising the little guys, so handsome and so intelligent (just like their *great* uncle), and how Jason is maturing into fatherhood, career, and citizenship. These are the memories I took from my visits to Pensacola and they're what I'll always keep—that we were all young once and that we all seem to be staying young, I can't say how. By any account, these memories are precious mementos to have, along with loads of photographs, several books and pamphlets, and a decorative jar of Perdido Beach sand standing on my windowsill.

SCATTERED NOTES ON IRISH PLACES

Ireland—June, 1996

County Mayo

We entered Ballyhaunis from the west, along the road that leads from the Knock Shrine. This road—R323—is two lanes and quite spacious for an Irish road. The scenery is pastureland, overwhelmingly green and with a rugged touch that comes from the ubiquitous low granite walls that serve in place of fences. Along the way the road makes a few sharp turns, anyone of which, taken too rapidly, could propel the car amid startled herds of cows lying in the grass. Fortunately, the traffic was light. On one trip made around 11:00 PM we traveled the entire route from Ballyhaunis to Knock without passing or being followed by a single car.

On our six trips into Ballyhaunis on R323 no pedestrians were observed, or none that remains in memory. The only living beings we noted were the cows who fed close to the road. In this part of Ireland cows are as ubiquitous as rocks and only slightly more mobile.

The road offers more picturesque scenery when taken in the opposite direction, that is, when traveling to the west toward Knock. From that direction the western mountain ranges are visible, and a grand sight they are, even at twenty miles. In addition, the road rides in places a little higher than the northern landscape, revealing a series of small lakes. In the long Irish evening it is a most beautiful and becalming sight to observe these lakes lying perfectly blue and still amid the lush greenness. You're in a hurry, because you're on the road, and everyone on Irish roads is in a hurry, but seeing these tranquil lakes has the effect of a pleasant day dream. It makes you want to pull to the side and let a few years pass before you continue on the trip. In olden times the *good people* might cooperate and put you to sleep for a spell; in our manic era even beings endowed with magical powers can't catch up.

Our connection to R323 was just to the north of the Knock Shrine. The Shrine is a religious complex dating from an apparition of the Blessed Mother to fifteen people on a rainy August evening in 1879. The parish was a dirt-poor place in 1879. Since that time it has become a place of pilgrimage to the faithful from all over Ireland and the world. Perhaps the most famous pilgrim was John Paul II, who made the journey early in his pontificate.

The grounds of the Shrine run for many acres. The church where the apparition occurred is on the road. The church is unremarkable except for a glass-enclosed chamber built in front of the gable wall. This chamber commemorates the exact place of the apparition. A statue of Mary stands to the left of an altar. At Mary's sides are statues of St. Joseph and St. John the Evangelist, both of whom appeared in the apparition. Behind them on the gable wall is a sculpture of an altar on which a lamb lies. Higher on the wall is a cross around which are representations of angels.

A mass was in progress while we visited. I suppose a mass is in progress nearly every hour of the day.

Behind the church is an immense circular Cathedral built at the time of the pope's visit. The building is not particularly attractive. The interior is thoroughly modern in design. Raised high off the floor, the altar is at the center of a vast semi-circle of seats. Many of the seats are built into the structure and can be referred to as "pews", but there are a large number of folding chairs as well. The entrances to the Cathedral are to the sides of the altar, so that the visitor encounters at first sight an ocean of seats. I suppose someone arriving late to mass is treated to an extraordinary spectacle. On second thought, I doubt that many people arrive late for mass.

The grounds to the Shrine are beautifully kept. There's a small pond below the Cathedral and a cemetery at the rear of the grounds. The cemetery is on a hill and holds an impressive number of tall and sculptured monuments near the entrance. Late in the afternoon the spikes of the monuments cross the blades of the devil's smile piercing the blue-edged cumulus clouds and bestow solemnity on the soul.

Near the southern end of the Knock complex is a wonderful folk museum. This museum, which can be entered for a small fee, includes recreations of peasant life in the nineteenth century. The ancestors didn't seem to have it so bad, according to the recreations I saw—no dung heaps at the doorway, no cows in the kitchen—but I think the downplaying of adversity was for the benefit of tourists, who have an idealized image of great-grandpappy and his family. As might be expected, Church history is prominently featured, including vestments belonging to Archbishop John McHale, a controversial cleric in his day.

Between the churches and the museum is a path on which pilgrims make the Stations of the Cross. It was midway on this path, along about the Sixth Station, that we had the most entertaining encounter of our visit to Erin. Standing at the station was a stout, black-haired gentleman of around forty years. He wore black trousers and coat and a thick black sweater. He carried a large duffel bag, also black. He looked at me and I looked at him and I knew I was going to have *the touch* laid on me just as Veronica was about to wipe the face of Jesus.

"Good afternoon, Father," I said.

"Good afternoon. Have you a tract concerning Our Lady of Knock?" He pulled a holy card from the duffel bag. It was a representation of Our Lady of Guadalupe.

I reached in my pocket for a donation. I was unfamiliar with Irish coins and fumbled with my fingers to find a donation that wasn't embarrassingly small or embarrassingly large.

"Are you not from here?" he asked.

"We're from New Jersey." He looked a little confused, so I added, "We live just across the river from New York City."

"That would be America. You have a truly fine cardinal in Cardinal Cushing."

"It's Cardinal O'Connor."

"He's cardinal of the great Cathedral on Third Avenue."

"It's Fifth Avenue."

"It's the Cathedral of St. Peter and Paul."

"It's St. Patrick's Cathedral." It began to dawn on me that he wasn't a priest, but a pilgrim overwhelmed by religious preoccupations. I felt around in my pocket for a small donation.

"Have you then heard of the Sister Faustina?"

"We have not."

"Sister Faustina was a most holy woman whom God is sure to raise to sainthood. Let me give you her tract." He reached in the bag and handed me a tract. It was a representation of St. John Bosco. "Are you familiar with—dear me, who is that famous saint from Mexico?"

"There must be a lot of Mexican saints."

"He was a most beloved and holy man. He traveled widely and wrote many profound sermons. His greatest sermon concerns the Four Ecclesiastical Virtues."

He remembered three. At this point we took leave of this gentle, and rather flustered, pilgrim. I was two tracts heavier and a few coins lighter, but I was glad to be of service as he honed his proselytism on holy ground.

The houses at the western end of Ballyhaunis are boxes one or two stories in height lined up in close order. They look exceptionally narrow, so narrow a grown man could reach from wall-to-wall. The houses lack front porches, alleys, or gardens, and have an aged and rundown appearance. They resemble row houses in Greenwich Village in Manhattan or in the Willow Terrace in Hoboken. Unlike the American houses, which tend to be monotone in color, some of the buildings in Ballyhaunis are painted bright pinks and yellows. The effect is quite at variance with the general appearance of the district, and it is quite pleasing to the traveler. Seeing such warm colors at the entrance of a town makes travelers think they're among friends.

R323 becomes Main Street as it enters Ballyhaunis. It also narrows considerably, becoming what is really one lane—one lane for two lanes of traffic. This shrinkage becomes instantly frazzling to an American. You're sitting in the wrong side of the car, traveling on the wrong side of the road, and unexpectedly there is hardly any road left to travel. The situation isn't helped by the emergence of tractor trailers appearing in the swim like tarpons in a tropical tank. No wonder the side-view mirrors on Irish cars are collapsible.

What strikes an American, used to mean streets, is the silence on Irish roads. Despite the narrow roads, despite the haste, despite the presence of eighteen wheelers stuck on streets too small for four wheelers, nobody blows their horns. Still less do drivers lean out their windows and curse your genealogy. Instead, drivers sit in polite silence waiting for the bottleneck to clear.

One characteristic that immediately impresses the traveler is the absence of door numbers. You enter Ballyhaunis, but without knowing whether you're in the high-numbered or low-numbered end of town. I remember driving back-and-forth on Main Street looking for Number 232, the residence of Alex Eaton. I found it only by pulling over and asking a pedestrian if he could direct me to Number 232. He couldn't, but he could direct me to where Alex Eaton lived. We drove to the opposite end of town and had an enjoyable conversation with Alex and his mother Josie, with whom Great-aunt Delia Forde lived for many years.

The Church of St. Patrick rises at the center of town on the south side of Main Street. St. Patrick's was built in 1908, so it was erected some years after the baptism of my grandfather, Pat Ford. (Pat was baptized in the Logboy chapel in southern Annagh Parish.) There were, however, many rites performed for the Fordes at St. Patrick's and Delia must have walked many the day to this church from her home with the Eatons.

St. Patrick's stands in what Americans call "the shopping district". On both sides of the street is a stretch of family-run stores and eateries. I recall a few five-and-dime stores; linens, glassware, and household goods are the usual fares. One such store was *Forde's*, strategically placed at the corner of Main and Knox Streets. In olden times this was "Market Square", where the cattle fair was held. Mr. Forde, the current proprietor, is not a relative; his ancestry lies in a different part of Mayo. He was, however, quite interested in genealogy.

One of the greatest surprises we experienced in Ballyhaunis occurred on Knox St. across from *Forde's*. I parked the little red rental on the wrong side of the street and observed a turbaned Mid-Easterner standing at the entrance of his store. He looked like a Sikh; he may have been Muslim. I was confused seeing such a person in such an obscure place as Knox St. in Ballyhaunis. For a moment I thought I had parked on Newark Ave. in Jersey City.

There are several food stores on Main St., including a bakery and a meat market. I observed only one store that could pass for an American-style supermarket. I stopped in and bought a few donuts, a bag of chips, and two beers to take back to the St. Thomas Bed & Breakfast in Knock—I cannot travel anywhere without donuts, chips, and beer. This market had a rear entrance that opened to a back street. This street was much more rundown than Main St. and contained a shell of a burnt building.

There are several restaurants on Main St. None can be considered a fast-food joint, which is quite the disappointment to a hungry traveler in a hurry. Several amounted to no more than storefronts containing a table or two. The top restaurant in town looked to be Val's, which was organized in the American fashion, with a large bar at the front, a dining room in the rear, and rapid service. I found Irish food simple and substantial. As might be expected, potatoes in various forms and sizes accompany every meal, including pasta dishes. Irish bread is especially tasty and appears in an amazing variety. Lasagnas are featured on the menus—it may be they get visitors from Rome making the rounds of holy wells.

It was in Val's that we met my cousins, Pat and Kathleen Hunt, and Kathleen Fitzharris of Derrynacong, the Forde ancestral townland. We were soon joined by the Hunts' daughters, Mary. Later, we traveled together to Derrynacong and then to the Hunts' home for a pleasant afternoon of conversation. Pat is a middle-aged gentleman who is descended from Michael Hunt, my great-grandmother's brother. His wife is descended from a Flynn family from Laughil, County Roscommon. (Laughil is where the Hunts resided in the nineteenth century.) Kathleen Fitzharris is a descendant of William Quinn, who shared property in rundale with Pat Forde, my great-great-grandfather, in Derrynacong. On and off, with no known marriages or debts, descendants of the Ford and Fitzharris families have been in contact for one hundred and fifty years. This is truly an astonishing fact that makes our families neighbors across space and time.

St. Mary's Abbey is the most famous and historic place in Ballyhaunis. According to tradition a Norman lord named Jordan Duff MacCostelloe donated the land to the Augustinian Friars in the fifteenth century. MacCostelloe was a local warlord whose family controlled the area until the end of the sixteenth century, when they were swindled out of the land by Theobald Dillon, the first Viscount Dillon—or *Discount Villain*, as a wit once observed. The area was the site of frequent skirmishes among various petty chieftains. The name Ballyhaunis derives from the Irish *Beal-atha-hambnois*, meaning "ford of the combat".

The Augustinians took possession in 1641. They held the Abbey until the end of the twentieth century, when the order ran out of Augustinians. Legend has it that the friars were originally attracted to the hill by the mysterious ringing of a bell. The church grounds now serve as a heritage center.

The Abbey was burned in one of Cromwell's rampages. Two friars were slain on the grounds and are buried near the eastern gable. Perhaps because of the isolation of the Abbey, friars were able to continue to say Sunday mass on the grounds during the Penal Times in the eighteenth century. During those years the Abbey served as the residence of the archbishop of the Tuam diocese. Only a small portion of the original church walls exist. The Abbey itself is remarkably small—it's not much larger than the "barn churches" that dot the Protestant countryside in America. The exterior walls are white and windowless. There are two altars inside and a small room that holds a display of assorted statues and monuments.

The Abbey sits atop a rather steep hill. There are two entrances from Main St. The larger entrance is a narrow paved road. The smaller one is a footpath leading from the west. Below the footpath is a small brackish stream. Somewhere nearby was a mill in olden times. The mill was in ruins before the Famine.

The Abbey—Friarsground, as it is called—is a holy place, rich in history and in family history. Until the 1880s the Abbey was the only consecrated burial ground in Annagh Parish. Countless thousands lie in the grass to the north and east of the church. My own people rest on the hill, sleeping like their compatriots in unmarked graves.

The solemn, rather melancholy atmosphere—of the tragedies visited on the Irish people for five centuries, of the inevitable deaths of individual ancestors—is intensified by an old and nearly ruined section of tombstones standing crookedly behind the church. Perhaps this section was demarcated for the people who could afford to risk the sin of pride by erecting monuments. Unfortunately, many of the people in this section have joined their poorer neighbors in the oblivion of namelessness. Many graves are in ruins. Headstones lie toppled and names etched in stone are erased by the elements and by the passage of time. Rows of graves are built on the declivity of the hill and grass devours the stones gravity leaves alone.

There is another cemetery in Ballyhaunis with significance to our family history. This is the "New Cemetery", which was established in the 1880s but not inhabited until slightly later. The story goes that no one wanted to be the first person to be buried there, so the place was empty of graves for a number of years.

The New Cemetery is raised from the roadway and designed in a rectangular shape. The cemetery sits in a much broader field perhaps double its size. I do not know if this field is reserved for possible expansion of graves. There is a clearly marked stone border separating the burial ground from the field, so perhaps the latter is private property.

What strikes the traveler as unique about Irish cemeteries is the uneven states of the graves. Unlike the American system, in which the cemetery takes responsibility for keeping the graves, the Irish system delegates this responsibility to the family. This can lead to esthetic offenses if the departed has no family or if survivors prefer not to be reminded of their mortality by dusting off headstones. So, in the New Cemetery, as in other cemeteries we visited, one can find graves in perfect repair standing next to graves in perfect disrepair. On one grave rests holy water and a bouquet; next to it is a grave hugged only by the wind. One grave is swept clean, the grass kept trim, with flowers planted to soften the harshness; next to it is a grave concealed by grass and weeds grown amuck. One grave stands erect and wears holy pictures and rosary beads; next to it lists a grave dressed in lichen.

Great-aunt Delia Forde and her fraternal twin Kate Flynn are buried together in a grave that borders the northern wall of the cemetery. Their plot is covered with small stones rather than with grass—probably a good choice, considering the Irish system. Their headstone is constructed of a thin white stone—probably a bad choice, since the stone has begun to stain. At the top of the stone is a tribute to their parents, Tom and Mary Forde.

Mary Forde, daughter of Pat and Bridget Hunt, born 1854, dead of tuberculosis in 1897, is most likely buried with her father in the cemetery in Garralahan parish, County Roscommon. Tom Forde, son of Pat and Bridget Forde, born 1856, dead of old age in 1939, is buried in an unmarked grave in the New Cemetery, most likely in the older section close to the road. There was a flag marking the grave at one point, but it was lost long ago. Delia tried to locate the grave in her old age and I made inquiries to County Mayo and to the local caretaker, but cemetery records go back only to the 1970s. It was a disappointment not to have located Tom's grave. I can say an *Ave* for him anywhere in the cemetery and, if I said enough of them, I would eventually stand in the right spot, but there is something decidedly final, after so long a journey, in finding the exact resting places of one's ancestors.

One of the major themes of the Irish experience is that of departure and return—rather, of departure and the yearning to return. This theme is seen at the start of Irish history, in Patrick's escape from slavery and return as a missionary. It is seen in the terribly repetitive upheavals in the Norman and English invasions. It is seen in the mass emigration in Famine times and throughout the rest of the nineteenth century. And it is seen in the lives of individual Irishers and descendants of Irishers—in my life, for example. It's true I never left, and a person who never left a place can hardly be said to return to it. Still, there's a sense of a home revisited after a long absence.

I'm the world's foremost authority on the nineteenth century social history of the townland of Derrynacong and I spent all of a half hour there in the spring of 1996. I don't think there's anything unusual in this. There are scientists who are experts on the outer planets of the solar system and they haven't spent any time—not so much as a half hour—on them. And there are scientists who claim to know what happened in the first seconds of the existence of the universe and they weren't even born yet.

We approached Derrynacong from Ballyhaunis, traveling to the north on a country road just wide enough for a file of cows or compact cars. Generally in good repair, these country roads are continuous with the lay of the land. There are no curbs, no sewers, no painted lines, no sign posts, no stop signs, and no directions. The roads run through field, forest, and bog. They run through ploughed fields and unploughed fields. They run through tilth and pasture. They run through groves so heavily overgrown, it's like driving through a natural tunnel. They run through grassy slopes of towering treeless hills so spacious, several counties are open to the glance.

Derrynacong is laid out in the modern style of private property and widely spaced homesteads. The term the Irish use is "striped", an event that happened here in the late 1850s; previous to this, property in Derrynacong was held in "rundale", which means it was shared among families or small groups of distantly related people. The houses that we saw are modern in appearance and set back from the road a good ways. The land is brilliantly green and reserved for pasture. Every now and then, it's broken by thick groves, "clumps" we call them in America, the most famous of which stands at Gettysburg. Strangely enough, this part of Mayo reminded me of southeastern Pennsylvania. Both places are a mix of rough and cultivated land flecked with galena-colored stones.

The site of the Forde farm is now pastureland owned by a gentleman named Ronanye, who lives nearby. Access to the property is gained by climbing a small wire fence—several cows were grazing the day I scaled it. The ground rises steeply from the road and flattens out. At the top of the incline, just over the fence, it is not possible to see the road.

The Forde home stood at the center of three widely spaced trees maybe fifty yards from the fence. If there's anything missing in Ireland other than snakes, it's trees, so I found it gratifying to see three at the heart of the Forde ancestral property.

Of course, the land looks quite different now than when the Fordes resided there. They had a stone house with a wood or thatch ceiling—the house "went under" in the 1960s. There was a barn near the house and a lime kiln some yards away. The kiln suggests the house was well built, since lime can serve as a substitute for cement. There was a path leading from the house to the road—maybe the land was flatter then. Turf for the hearth was obtained at the opposite end of the property in the direction of the townland of Arderry.

When the family was together, the farm must have been a lively place. Probably, it was a contentious place. Two stepfamilies and eight children separated in age by sixteen years. One boy—my grandfather—and seven girls. That sounds like trouble. We were told Pat left Ireland because of Bridget Lyons, his evil stepmother, but there may have been other females involved in his decision. There would have been chickens and cows and pigs roaming about. The potato patch and the vegetable garden were close to the house; a little ways out was pasture for the cows that paid the rent with their lives. Tom and Pat would have been busy with the livestock and with the heavier chores. The girls would have tended the gardens and the chicken coops. And the unfortunate Bridget Lyons would be lurking at the fringes of this tumultuous scene baring claws, fangs, and a red apron spotted with ill will.

My visit to Derrynacong was all too brief, but I couldn't have my hosts wait on my daydreams for an unduly long period and I became aware of the unsettling fact that several bulky cows were eyeing me rather observantly. We were told Irish cows are friendly, but you can't believe everything you hear.

After we visited Derrynacong we drove to the Hunt ancestral site located in the Roscommon townland of Laughil. This sounds like a lengthy trip, but Laughil is on the border with Mayo and is no more than a few minutes drive from Derrynacong.

Laughil is the tiniest and most picturesque of my ancestral Irish townlands. It lies in Kiltullagh Parish near the crest of one of the hills that runs southward from Ballyhaunis. Access is along a lane that leads imperceptively upward. Only at the townland itself is there the experience of actual height. It's a characteristic of Irish hills that travelers rarely have the experience of ascent. Probably, the absence of trees and the resultant wide spaces mask the sensation of climbing. And it may be that tourists are too busy looking to note how far they've traveled. But I guess that's one of the morals of life—we never realize how far we've traveled until the journey ends.

Laughil consists of three or four modern homes. The Forde home is lowest, near where the road turns—it is at the point where you realize how high up you are. On the right is the Flynn home. The Grennan property is higher up. I have many connections, now and in the long ago, to this tiny place. The Fordes of Derrynacong were connected in some manner to the Fordes of Laughil, but no living person knows how. Mr. Flynn is brother to Kathleen Hunt, who's married to a descendant of my great-great-grandfather, who *married into* Laughil in 1853. And the Grennans are descended from the Hamrock family, one of whom (Henry) was Tom Forde's godfather.

The Hunt property was opposite Mr. Flynn's house—we really can't say it was "across the street". The property was quite small and housed two large families—Pat Hunt's family and that of his brother-in-law, Pat Fitzmaurice. All told, something like fourteen people lived on a few acres. Fourteen people, two houses, and four rooms. They must have used bunk beds or slept in shifts.

No one has resided on the property since 1910, when the Hunts left. The land is now heavy with turf. A fence, standing about waist high, marks the edge alongside the road. Near the fence is a stump of a tree, cut level with the ground. Another fence, or some kind of enclosure, runs outward into the field; this enclosure is concealed with thick vines and weeds. To the rear, some ways up the hill and curving with the property, is a stone wall. Behind the wall is County Mayo. There is a memory among the people here that three bodies were found at this wall in Famine times.

County Kerry

In some ways Ballybunion resembles Keansburg, New Jersey, a small-town resort on Raritan Bay across the water from Coney Island. The houses are plain, constructed mostly of drab whites or clay colors and seldom more than two stories in height. Restaurants, pubs, stores, even a casino or two—everything is within a two or three block walk. And small blocks they are, too.

The center of town is Lower Main Street. Here the traveler finds the amusements expected in a "resort". There are several fine restaurants, all keeping limited hours. There are a number of pubs, all dark and dreary in the daylight. Outside one of the pubs is an outdoor liquor store. For an exorbitant amount a traveler can ease his journey with a six-pack of wets. Chips can be purchased at the local convenience store. So can an awful-tasting seaweed snack.

Further along Lower Main St.—this is about as low as one can go before falling into the sea—is the general store owned by Mr. J. J. O'Carroll. Mr. O'Carroll is descended from the John Allen who resided in my ancestral townland of Ballyegan in the long ago. This probably makes us very distant relatives—the emphasis is on the word "very". Mr. O'Carroll is a pleasant gentleman of about seventy. He was kind enough to take an interest in genealogy, inviting us into his store for a long discussion. He gave us a copy of a photo of his relatives, several of whom settled in Canada.

Part of the problem in Irish genealogy is that everyone has the same name. (This is the inverse of the situation in Polish genealogy, in which no two people have the same name.) So, all nineteenth century male Allens were John, Patrick, or Henry. All the female Allens were Johanna or Mary. This doesn't make it easy for very distant cousins to sort out who's related to whom. I don't think it made it easy to sort things out in the nineteenth century. When someone called out "John" or "Johanna", any number of people could have responded.

Mr. O'Carroll's store is close to what in the old days was called Station Road, the Ballybunion terminus of that strange one-wheel railroad that ran from Listowel, the parish town. Timothy Allen, my grand-uncle—my great-grandmother's brother—resided nearby and was employed as a ticket agent for the railroad. Timothy was the only one of my great-grandmother's siblings who did not immigrate to the States. We didn't know it during this visit, but two of his grandchildren lived just around the corner from Mr. O'Carroll.

Ballybunion most assuredly differs from Keansburg in two respects. There is no amusement park and the natural grandeur of the place overwhelms sights in New Jersey. (The only thing New Jersey has going for it in comparison is sand, and plenty of it.) Ballybunion sits atop a truly impressive rock formation—the ocean is literally ten stories below you. These cliffs run from the mouth of the Shannon River a few miles to the north at Beale Point to the Cashen River a few miles to the south. It's possible to walk along the edge of the cliffs. There are the ruins of a small medieval fort along the way and a hole in the stone path where, the story goes, a bad-tempered Viking lord threw several of his daughters to death. The view of the ocean is terribly impressive from the top of the cliffs—we don't get so grand a view in Wildwood Crest.

The beach—*strand*, the Irish say—is bordered at the north by the massive base of the rock formation. It's not possible to walk around the cliffs. You need a boat to explore the coastline—it would have to be a good-size boat, as the surf is rough, constantly banging against the rocks. There are caves in the cliff walls beside the beach, but they go only a few feet in and are more like indentations than true caves. At the entrance of the beach is a small, dingy-looking building that offers a seaweed bath, but we didn't avail ourselves of the opportunity. The seaweed in the tub is a long, thick strap of a plant that could do some damage if mishandled.

We were standing on the northern beach, which was reserved for men in the chaste times of the past. The southern beach, which was where the women congregated, is separated from it by a peninsula of rock that juts onto the sand. Atop this peninsula are the ruins of the medieval castle belonging to the Fitzmaurice family. These ruins are Ballybunion's emblem and are featured on postcards and guidebooks. All that's left of the castle is a single wall that offers no defense against the wind—it looks impressive for being so thin and lonely and it looks a little odd, being a wall placed in the middle of a vast expanse of openness. I don't doubt that it has frequently been rebuilt over the years.

The fact that the men and women stayed on different beaches may be the reason why the Irish are such strong swimmers.

We had heard that every field and square inch of every townland in Ireland has a name. This is not true, apparently, of large, imposing buildings that dominate the landscape for far and wide.

The parish church in Ballybunion is an intimidating building built of dark stones and with a castle-like tower. It stands on an elevated parcel of land two blocks from the coast road. There is a cemetery behind the church. The cemetery grounds are kept up nicely.

Of course, we inspected the interior of the church. With no disrespect, it must have been a nondescript place, since I have no memory of the interior. Being inquisitive Americans, we wanted to know the name of the church— for the record. There were no informative posters outside or bulletins lying in the pews. We asked a person who was kneeling in the rear for the name. Amazingly, this person did not know the name of the church he was in. I'm not sure he understood the question. "Tis the church," is what he said.

We walked across the street to a small store. We call this kind of place a "candy store" in America. We asked the lady seated at the cash register for the name of the church across the street. I do mean, literally, *across the street*. She didn't know. "'Tis the church," she said.

I didn't believe for a moment that we had found the church with no name. And I didn't believe the name of the church was "the church". The post office would have trouble with letters addressed to the rectory of "The Church of The Church." I can't imagine the people are ashamed to say the name of their church. I conjectured the name of the saint may have been unpronounceable or that the saint resided in the upper deck, or maybe even in the bleachers, of the ballpark where the canonized reside.

We found out later—I'm not sure how, but somebody must have let it slip—that the church had a name. And a fine name it was—The Church of St. John. Still, 'tis passing strange that two residents didn't tell us. It must have been the question or how we phrased it. Maybe it was our accents. I hate to think they didn't want to tell us.

NEW JERSEY PILGRIMS VISIT THE NEW ZION

Utah—June, 2002

June 11

The heart of Salt Lake City and the soul of Mormonism is Temple Square. It's like the Vatican to a Catholic or Mecca to a Muslim. It's a place every Mormon visits, or wants to visit, and a lot of people who aren't Mormons visit there, too.

We visited Temple Square for the first time late Tuesday afternoon. It's a ten-minute drive from the Day's Inn where we lodged. On this visit we parked in the ZCMI Mall, located across the street from the Square. This mall is sponsored by the church to counter the sprawl of suburban malls everywhere else in Salt Lake City. It's quite modest in scale, with only a few pricey stores. The bottom floor of the mall is a food court.

Temple Square is ten acres in size. It consists of thirteen buildings. The centerpiece is, of course, the massive Temple, which is the holiest place in the Mormon faith. It is so holy non-Mormons are not allowed to enter. To get inside you have to be a Mormon in "good standing". I'm not sure what it means to be a Mormon in good standing—possibly it has something to do with financial contributions. Whatever it is, I would guess that a considerable number of Mormons are not allowed to enter. I've always found this an odd situation, that the most sacred site is forbidden to outsiders. This would be comparable to the Vatican being off limits to everyone but Catholics or to a subset of Catholics in good with the pope. It's no wonder conspiracy theorists have asked, *"Just what the heck goes on inside?" "Do they really slay virgins?" " Do they really drink blood?" "Do they really communicate with the Dark Lords?"*

Work on the temple began on April 6, 1853. It was completed forty years later on April 6, 1893. The architect was Truman O. Angell, who was commissioned by Brigham Young.

The walls to the temple are fortress thick—they are nine feet at ground level. The building stands 210 feet tall and is light gray in appearance. There are three massive pillars on each end, each concluding in a spire. On the middle spire on the eastern side a gold statue of the Angel Moroni stands—Moroni is the angel who delivered the Book of Mormon to Joseph Smith.

Immediately behind the temple is the Tabernacle, home to the world-famous choir. The Tabernacle is the oldest functioning building in Temple Square, having been completed in 1867. The building has unique acoustical qualities owing to its wooden dome. You can literally hear a pin drop at a distance of 170 feet. I wouldn't have believed it, if I didn't hear it with my two good ears.

The Tabernacle is deceptively tiny. From the outside it appears to be a small structure, but it's not. The building is shaped so that it descends into the ground. It can hold more than two thousand people, including the choir, who sit on steeply raised pews along both sides of a flower-draped altar. Men are to the right, women to the left. The organ is considered a masterpiece—it has 11,623 pipes, enough pipes to cause Garth Hudson to become afflicted with carpal tunnel syndrome. Entrance is directly into the auditorium. There is no vestibule. There is no admission fee. The audience is not segregated by gender.

The spiritual heart of Temple Square may lie inside the Temple, but the social heart lies in front of the Tabernacle. Tourists congregate here and so do a number of good-looking young Mormons, all of whom offer tours of the temple grounds. There's no guessing who the Mormons are and who the tourists are. We are in Temple Square, after all. Even if we weren't, it's easy to spot a Mormon. The Mormons in Utah look exactly like the Mormons we met at the Family History Library in Manhattan—clean, tidy, well-dressed, polite, and immaculately wholesome.

We were given the tour by two Sisters, one from Seattle, the other from Arizona.

In many ways the most interesting building—the warmest in human terms—is Assembly Hall, which is to the left of the Tabernacle. Assembly Hall was completed in 1882 using sandstone and granite leftover from the construction of the Temple. There are beautiful ornate doors that align with the Sea Gull Monument for outstanding photographs. The interior resembles what we might think of as a prototypical Protestant church—simple wood pews, a balcony, a huge organ consisting of wood and copper pipes, a gold-colored ceiling, and forty stained-glass windows.

The Sea Gull Monument was erected in 1913 to commemorate the 1848 near-disaster in which an invasion of crickets started to consume the harvest. Miraculously, a herd of gulls arrived in answer to prayers and consumed the crickets, breakfast, lunch, and dinner. We told our guides that, as New Jersey residents, we were quite familiar with sea gulls. They were not familiar with the species of laughing gull that inhabits The Shore in summer.

The tour concludes at the North Visitor Center. Inside, they give you a slightly harder sell about the Mormon Church. I have never been tempted to join, although the possibility of slaying virgins does slightly tempt me. There is an eleven-foot statue of Christ in a second-floor rotunda room. Statues of Adam and Eve are in an adjoining room, as well as a passage with murals depicting scenes from the Bible.

In the North Visitor Center we encountered for the first time a phenomenon that must be unique to Salt Lake City. This is the phenomenon of "seated Mormons". Wherever we went—no matter what building, floor, or corridor—there were sure to be Mormons seated in the vicinity. Sometimes, they served as obvious security checkpoints. Other times, they were seated in places that didn't appear remotely strategic. No matter, they were unfailingly polite; usually, they were on the senior side of life. They tended to be mixed sexes, probably husbands and wives. They invariably broke the ice with the phrase, "Why, you're not from around here." If you didn't tell them, they made it a point to guess where you were from.

After our tour we returned to the motel for a rest and then drove back into town for dinner at an Italian restaurant called Baci-Trattoria on West Pierpont Ave. I had a vegetable ziti dish and Babci had shrimp linguini.

The big news in Salt Lake City during our visit was the kidnapping of a fourteen-year-old girl named Elizabeth Smart. She was abducted on June 5. Incredibly, she was found unharmed on March 12, 2003, having spent the interval in a way-out religious cult. (In Utah, this means *way out*.) Elizabeth has withdrawn into obscurity, but her father remains a public advocate for the safety of children.

June 12

After a restful night we proceeded to the Family History Library, which is the Bowling Green of knowledge for family historians.

The world headquarters of genealogy is located in an unpretentious gray building across the street from the Tabernacle. The Library is adjacent to a sister building that serves as a museum of the Mormon Church. An attractive promenade lined with lush flowers separates the buildings. The promenade leads to the parking lot at the rear. The procedure for paying for parking is one of those delightful Mormon eccentricities. Once you select a numbered parking space, you proceed to what looks to be a row of mailboxes. You find the number that corresponds to the parking space and insert three dollars in the slot. If you have trouble inserting the bills, there's a spatula that hangs from the side of the boxes. Everyone is on the honor system, but I doubt that genealogists travel all the way to Utah to stiff the church of three dollars on the hollowed ground of the Mother of all Family History Libraries.

The phenomenon of seated Mormons is amply demonstrated in the Library. There's a station at the entrance where seated Mormons greet family historians and, for that matter, anyone who happens to wander in. They say with all sincerity, "Why, you're not from around here." Since very few people are "from around here", they must say the same greeting hundreds of times daily. If you're new to genealogy, you're directed to an orientation room. If you're a pro, or if you look like you know where you're going, you can proceed to a second station where other seated Mormons direct you further, after noting, "Why, you're not from around here."

The first and second floors are devoted to American genealogy. There's a large copy room on the second floor. We arrived at the Library early, so these floors were empty. By the end of the day, they were so crowded, it was difficult to find seats.

An elevator is located to the right of the entrance—it's impossible to get on or off the elevator without acknowledging, "Yes, we're not from around here." Basement One is devoted to European and International research. There's a large area devoted to published books on this floor. Unfortunately, the pickings were slim in Polish and Lithuanian genealogy. Basement Two is devoted exclusively to British and Irish genealogy. Basement Two was our destination.

Basement Two is rectangular in shape. The short wall near the elevator holds rest rooms and a copy center. The area near the far wall houses bookshelves, and wonderful books they hold, too. The long wall to the left contains lockers and reference books. The long wall to the right consists of hundreds of vertical and horizontal drawers. The drawers hold the sacred objects of Irish genealogy, thousands and thousands of reels of microfilm arranged in perfect numerical order. The procedure was pretty much the same as in Manhattan. You find comfortable chairs, readers with bright bulbs, get your tapes, and settle down to the hunt.

We were able to examine (and photocopy) the 1911 Census for the Ballybunion, County Kerry, vicinity, which was a major objective for the trip from New Jersey to the New Zion. The major discovery was finding that Ellen Griffin, my great-grandmother, was a widow since 1903 and that she had an additional child, heretofore unknown, who was not alive in 1911. And we saw the handwriting of my great-great grandfather, John Allen, on the Census Form.

We had lunch at the food court in the Crossroads Mall and supper at an Oriental restaurant called Café Trang. This restaurant is well-regarded in Salt Lake City, but we had a difficult time locating it. *Frommer's Guide* had the right address, but the wrong location on the map. They had it placed near the State Capitol; in fact, it was on the other side of town. We discovered this after driving in circles for the better part of an hour. The State Capitol, by the way, was built in 1915 and is a replica of the United States Capitol on a smaller scale. The capitol stands on a steep hill overlooking the city. The neighborhood is very upscale—this must be the heart of upper-class Mormonism. Across from the capitol there is a park called Memory Grove. It is located in a steep ravine and is a tribute to Utahan veterans and, in an odd combination, to the Liberty Bell.

I suppose the drive was worth the aggravation. Café Trang turned out to be the culinary highlight of the trip. I had a dish entitled *Dau hu Sot ca Chua*, otherwise known as "Crisp Fried Bean Curd Simmered in Tomato Sauce", and I can testify it tasted a lot better than its name. There were three intoxicated businessmen at a table near us. Like all men who are blotto, they were talking excessively loud. And they were talking about what seemed at first hearing a most unsavory topic in a restaurant—about "dumps" and "dumping". I was pretty offended, until I realized they were talking about computer data and not about what I thought they were referring to.

Contrary to the guidebook and to Utah's reputation as a *dry* state, liquor flowed plentifully in all the restaurants we dined in. Unless there were hidden charges, I didn't notice any "club fees" that had to be paid in order to sip Bacchos. There even was a large liquor store on the way to Temple Square.

June 13

Babci and I returned to the Family History Library, where we focused on the 1911 Census for the vicinity of Ballyhaunis, County Mayo. We found Anne

Forde, living with her Lyons grandparents in the townland of Larganboy, and possibly Kate Forde, residing with the Cribben family in Moneymore, We weren't able to locate Delia or Mary Ellen, who remains the lost sheep of the family.

We then crossed Temple Square and proceeded to the twenty-sixth floor observation deck located atop the Mormon Office Building. The trail upward is exquisitely organized. Mormons are seated everywhere, except for the hostess who accompanied our group to the observation deck. I was able to take some outstanding photographs of the Temple and of the State Capital.

We proceeded to the Crossroads Mall, which is touted in the tour book. But that's a tall tale. I found the Mall disappointing. I bought an introductory guide for converts in the Deseret Bookstore, not that I would convert, although the idea of parading around in "Temple undergarments" sounds intriguing. Later, I bought a crystal Christ in a handicrafts store located on the street outside the mall.

We had dinner at the Garden Restaurant, which is on the tenth floor of the Joseph Smith Memorial Building located across the street from Temple Square. This is an old hotel shaped roughly like the letter H. It has a gorgeous green glass lobby and plenty of seated Mormons. I had vegetable lasagna, which was heavy on the cheese, and Babci had grilled chicken.

That evening, we heard a rehearsal of the Mormon Tabernacle Choir. They were already in place when the audience was allowed to walk in. They focused on two songs, "Hosanna", which was sung in 1893 when the Temple was finished, and an older song that sounded like "Stir the Fire", which is sung whenever a new temple is opened. They are up to number 113 in the United States.

I have never been in a place more pedestrian friendly than Salt Lake City. A sign at the 200 South block near the Family History Library advises pedestrians to look both ways before crossing and, if they need it, to take an orange flag available in a bucket on the street pole and wave it as they proceed. If they make it across, they have to place the flag in the receptacle on the other side. Starting at seventeen seconds, the "Walk" sign flashes the time pedestrians have till they're sent over hoods to the particular judgment. Chimes ring out the last few seconds.

The streets are exceptionally wide in this part of town, so slow-moving folk may need all the help they can get. The streets were laid out to be "wide enough for a team of four oxen and a covered wagon to turn around."

June 14

This is the third anniversary of Dad's passing—we are a long way today from 3247 Kennedy Blvd., Jersey City.

We drove on Route 15 South to Route 92, which leads in a circuitous course directly up and over the 11,750 foot Mount Timpanogos. Well, actually not up and over the top. More like up and over a hip of this giant. In places the road was little more than a single lane, just like the kind we see in movies.

Timpanogos is named for an Indian tribe that inhabited the place in the long ago, although there is a legend that the name is a composite for a Native American Romeo and Juliet. Supposedly, the name cannot be said aloud or lightning and thunder will break out. I know for a fact that this legend is not true, since I said Timpanogos—in fact, I shouted it, "There's Mount Timpanogos!"—and the sun kept smiling.

We stopped at the Sundance Lodge, which at six thousand feet is the midsection of the mountain. This is part of the Robert Redford conservation site. Sundance is a private community founded in 1969 as an "experiment in environmental stewardship and artistic expression". Or so the brochure claims, and I don't doubt it. There is a lodge, a bed-and-breakfast, a general store, a snack bar, and a full-service restaurant. We got a few snacks and sat for a while on benches located on the outside of the restaurant. I don't know what Babci was thinking, but I pretended I was a big-time Hollywood type. A short walk from the lodge takes you to a ski lift, which has a truly phenomenal view of the white head of the mountain. This is a hackneyed expression if there ever was one, but the view was postcard perfect, and I have the photograph to prove it.

As we toured the viewing sites on Timpanogos I noticed what I thought were butterflies. These turned out to be flying grasshoppers with red wings.

We then drove to Route 189, a major highway that runs through the Provo Canyon along the southern side of Timpanogos. The scenery in this place is spectacular. The land is flat and there are vast mountains in the distance, but it's hard to tell just what the distance is, given the range of vision and the dearth of nearby landmarks. If I were standing on the shore, I could say the mountains were at the *offing*. The mountains are blue and barren, almost desert-like. There's not a lot of green visible. One mountain is named Cascade, and it's a huge glinting hump of rock.

We found Route 15 and drove through Orem to a place called Thanksgiving Point, which is a combination educational center and tourist trap. There's a museum called the Museum of Ancient History, which mostly featured dinosaurs and cost $14.00 per person to tour. It did have an excellent gift shop. I bought a fossil insect and two trilobites.

After pausing for a malted milk at Thanksgiving Point, we continued north to Sandy, where Barnes & Noble has a store "in the parking lot", as the shipping labels say. We dined at a restaurant called Mayan at Jordan Commons, which is an upscale mall. The restaurant featured Mexican food and a show about Mayan gods. The tables are centered around a pool and rock façade three stories high. Buff dancers in various stages of undress acted out scenes from Mayan folklore, most of which ended with diving into the pool. Really, it was quite enjoyable and unique. And a little distracting, since it's hard to decide whether to eat or watch. I'm talented, but not that talented. It was hard to do both.

We then drove four miles from building #9400 to building #1 along South State St.. The ride was pretty much one long car dealership and shopping mall. Along the way I noticed motorcyclists don't wear helmets. This is a startling sight to someone from New Jersey, where you practically have to wear a helmet when you walk.

We stopped at the Family History Library on the way to the motel. After a ten-hour day our minds weren't on photocopying the 1838 Ordnance Maps on fiches, so we left after a few minutes.

June 15

The Great Salt Lake is easily accessible from Salt Lake City via I-95 and a county road that passes through a city called Syracuse. Antelope Island lies seven miles into the lake, but it, too, is easily accessible along a causeway that crosses the distance nearly level with the water. The interstate and county roads are free. The causeway costs $4.00. The view is worth more than $4.00.

The Great Salt Lake is an impressive site and it has an impressive history, although, like a lot of things in Utah, there's an oddness about the impressiveness. The lake we know today is a remnant of a much larger lake that existed more than fourteen thousand years ago. This prehistoric lake covered much of Northern Utah and extended into present-day Nevada and Idaho. The Great Salt Lake receives much of its water from four rivers. The southern river, named Jordan, connects with Lake Utah, which we glimpsed when we emerged from the mountains on our excursion to Mt. Timpanogos. But the Great Salt Lake is a dead end and has no outlet, which is the cause of the immense accumulation of salt and mineral deposits. This accumulation is responsible for a malicious odor near the start of the causeway in Syracuse. *Frommer's Guide* warned about the odor, and they weren't kidding. The odor is wicked enough to reanimate the dead, which is why they don't have cemeteries in Syracuse.

There are more than four billion tons of dissolved salt in the lake. Surprisingly, little table salt is produced, since the quality is uneven and production costs are prohibitive. Most of the salt harvested from the lake is used in industry and for road surfaces. Some is sold to tourists in little vials.

Because of the excessive saltiness, few animals live in the lake. The commonest species is a brine shrimp. Loads of wild birds live on the lake, though.

The lake measures seventy five miles by thirty five miles and has a surface elevation of 4,200 feet. The maximum depth is thirty three feet, although the water level varies greatly from season to season, given the changeable rates of flow from the four rivers. There are eleven islands in the lake. Antelope Island is, by far, the largest of the eleven.

When people think of lake islands they usually imagine lush green and tropical places with crowded beaches and boat slips and playgrounds. Antelope Island is nothing like that. It is a gray and grim place, with huge bald mountains rising an additional two thousand feet above sea level. Historically, herds of bison, sheep, and horses have roamed its trails. The island has stood in as a desert backdrop in movies, and it has served just fine in that role. It really resembles a desert, which makes sense, since the lake it rises from is a liquid desert.

There are signs warning of the dangers of wild animals such as bison—any sign that mentions "dangerous" and "bison" in the same sentence has to be taken seriously. But we didn't see any wild animals other than gulls, and we didn't have to leave New Jersey to see them. We didn't drive to the bison pens that are located near the center of the island. The road to the pens was in bad repair and we were running late.

Antelope Island roughly resembles a lopsided exclamation point, without the point. The northern tip of the island juts roundly into the lake, but with a chunk of the western border chewed off. This is White Rock Bay, a place where people stand in the water. This is another example of the pervasive oddness of the place, that no one actually enters such a huge body of water above the knees. The rest of the island tapers off in a southeasterly direction. The southernmost portion is separated from the mainland by a strip of water called Farmington Bay.

Antelope Island was first explored by John Fremont. Later in his career he became a failed presidential candidate and a failed Union general. Fremont named the island for the herds of antelope he saw romping.

The first official Caucasian settler was Fielding Garr, a Mormon, who started ranching on the southeastern section of the island in 1848. However, old records indicate that Garr had company in the person of the wonderfully named Daddy Stump, a mountain man who disappeared in the hard winter of 1855-56. No one knows what happened to Daddy Stump. It may be he died in the snow. It may be he moved on—after all, Antelope Island was getting to be a crowded place.

There's an attractive visitor's center at the northern end of the island. It contains a tiny museum detailing the geology and history of the area, as well as a small bookstore. I purchased an outstanding topographical map of the island and a pamphlet on local history. Like most local histories done by amateurs, this one was badly organized and cluttered with a vast number of superfluous details.

The drive to the Garr ranch is approximately ten miles from the visitor's center. The drive is along the eastern edge of the island—I do mean "edge". The scenery is impressive—the mountains on the mainland are big and blue across Farmingham Bay and the barren brownness of Antelope Island extends to the south. The mountains on Antelope Island possess a harsh, unforgiving quality. They look too near and, at the same time, too far away, like the end of a paddle studied at eye level must look to a child about to be whacked. The scenery toward the mainland was dreamy in a disconcerting sort of way, being at the same time mightily majestic and mighty empty. The day we visited was hot and humid. The longer I looked at the sights through the white haze of heat, the more difficult it became to define where the coastline began or where the mountains crested.

The paralyzing stillness was broken only by the movement of cars, which could be tracked for miles. Because of the flat terrain and the absence of trees, this movement possessed a cartoonish quality. The strangeness of the flow of the traffic may also have had to do with the fact that every driver kept to the posted speed—twenty five miles an hour. This was sensible, since the road in places was a few yards from the edge of the lake, with only gravity between the lug nuts and a corrosive wash.

The Garr ranch consisted of a collection of typical farm structures. There was a farmhouse, a barn, a maze of pens and corrals, and a number of small structures, some leading to subterranean pits used to store food. The ranch had been in continuous operation from 1848–1981, when the government purchased the area and turned it into a park. A portion of the farmhouse and a few of the pens were originals, which make them the oldest human-made structures in Utah.

Fielding Garr's ranch numbered as many as a thousand head of cattle. Subsequent ranch operations included sheep, horses, and bison. The purpose of the ranch was to raise funds for Mormon immigration into Utah. The herds didn't reside at the ranch, but roamed Antelope Island, as herds are wont to do. Seasonally, ranch hands would round them up, as ranch hands are wont to do. The hands traveled in covered wagons, one of which survives. We took some pictures and peeked in. To our surprise, the interior of the wagon was like the interior of a modern long-haul tractor, only more so. There was a bed, a tiny stove, and storage cabinets.

Frary Peak stands a few miles to the north of the Garr Ranch—at 6,596 feet it's the highest point in the range. The mountain is named for George Issac Frary, who lived at the base of the mountain and who ran an excursion boat on the lake in the nineteenth century. A steep road leads to an observation deck about a third of the way up. A hiking trail continues to the peak, if you're so inclined. We were not so inclined. The view is specta-ocular, except there's not much to see. You're so high up, and the island and the lake below are so devoid of features, and the light is so devilishly lacteal, there's nothing to see other than sheer distance—it is a distance devoid of angles. It's an immense circular loneliness coincidental with the squint in the corneas, but even bloodshot irises can't add color to a colorless slate.

A vicious outcropping of ancient black rock hangs near the observation post like a funeral verandah over a burial party. I don't like mountains and this feature of Frary Peak looked especially sinister. The outcropping resembles an emerging fist—the index finger is coming through first, pointed right at you. The mountain looms a few thousand feet over the deck, and it looks to be leaning over you. I felt like an insect must feel at the moment it's about to be swatted into oblivion. It doesn't help knowing that George Frary's wife, who died tragically young, is buried nearby.

I don't like mountains, but I do like rocks—this is my single vice as a tourist. I grabbed two reddish rocks lying at the edge of the observation post. These rocks resembled chunks of half-cooked roast beef.

Our final stop was Buffalo Point, located at the chewed-off portion of island on the northwestern side. At 4,785 feet Buffalo Point commands a fabulous—and slightly blurry—view of the northern end of Antelope Island. The visitor's center and causeway are visible to the east, as is Bridger's Bay, named for Jim Bridger, who is given credit for discovering the Great Salt Lake for Caucasians in 1824. White Rock Bay is to the west. This is a picturesque place, but very barren. From this height it's possible to track roads as they run off in the distance, like tan wrinkles in a tan hide. The water in White Rock Bay is bluish gray and still. It resembles soil more than it does water. A white wrack of salt, yards wide in places, demarcates the water from the land. This white crust is not unique to this part of the island, but rings the entire coast. However, it lies especially thick at White Rock Bay. There is no beach, as we sand-loving citizens of New Jersey understand beaches.

There's a small restaurant atop Buffalo Point and a well-stocked gift shop with an amazing variety of items, many at the high end of the price spectrum. I suppose the retail logic is that visitors are so worked up over the view, they will be inspired to buy souvenirs without regard to the prices. I've found that rocks are cheaper and last longer than store-bought souvenirs.

The salesladies were seated. I didn't ask, but the chances were very good they were Mormons.

We drove into Wyoming after our tour of Antelope Island. There was no particular purpose behind this drive, except that I could then tell people I was *in Wyoming.* We didn't get far into Wyoming, but we made it into Evanston, which is inside the border, so it counts.

Evanston is eighty-three miles from Salt Lake City. This is ninety minutes at seventy miles an hour. Ninety minutes once you get started, that is. We no sooner left the Great Salt Lake than we sat in a gigantic traffic jam on Route 15 in Ogden—or *Ogreden*, considering the bad mood I got in. Between arguments and grumpiness—most of the grumpiness was mine—I got to thinking about a dialogue that might have happened in these parts in the long ago.

Fielding Garr and Daddy Stump are on the range. It's a June evening in the year 1854. They are sitting near an open fire. Beans and bison bits are in the pan. A coffee pot, charred with use, is on the ground next to the fire. With apologies to the movie *My Cousin Vinnie*, Fielding is played by Fred Gwynne. Daddy Stump is played by Joe Pesci. He wears a thick gray hairpiece.

"So, Daddy, you're not from these parts?"

"No sir-ree. I'm from over them thar' hills."

"Who were the original people hereabouts?"

"Original people? You mean Adam and Eve?"

"No, the original people in these here parts—the parts we're sitting in."

"Oh, you mean who were the Injuns. They would be the Utes."

"The Utes?"

"Yes, the Utes."

"What's a Ute?"

As you can see, even the most stable mind becomes unhinged in traffic jams.

The road to Evanston was amazingly winding in places—it was like riding a series of slanted eights. Signs warn truckers not to exceed fifty five miles an hour, which is sensible advice for drivers of cars as well, given the reality of centrifugal forces. Most of the mountains resemble Timpanogos—they're huge and gray and somewhere far off in the distance. The rock formations that are closer to the highway are cheery yellow and fierce red in complexion; they are smaller in statue and weirdly shaped. I imagine they are how rock formations look in Southern Utah.

I'm sure it's a fine city, but we didn't get to see much of Evanston. We stayed just long enough for a quick snack at McDonald's. This was at the entrance of town, just off the interstate, so there were a lot of fast food places to choose from. I did walk around the parking lot and on the sidewalk, so I can officially say I stepped foot in the state of Wyoming.

The trip back to Salt Lake City was easy. The traffic was light. And it was all downhill. I do mean "downhill". I just kept my foot near the brake and let gravity do all the work—it didn't mind. The road looped and looped and curved and curved and finally dropped us in for a landing near Temple Square, which is where all roads in Utah end.

Our last evening in the New Zion was spent in the Redrock Café, a Cheers-like bar near the Baci-Trattoria. I had a portobello mushroom sandwich, Babci had pastrami. Both were superb.

MOUNT DORA, FLORIDA

July—2004

In one of O. Henry's short stories a traveling salesman has to spend a weekend in a nondescript hick town somewhere in the South. This salesman is a slick fellow and a sophisticate and he's convinced from the dismal look of things that the weekend will take a month to pass. There is no liquor in town, no dancing, no singing, no gambling, and no dames. He's sure he will die of boredom. He soon learns that this backwater place conceals terrible secrets of interracial love, rage, and murder.

That's fiction. This chapter highlights some of the story of Mount Dora, Florida, a nondescript hick town in the South where, apparently, nothing of any consequence has ever happened. Or so the published record claims.

How Mount Dora Got Its Name

Mount Dora is located in the northeastern portion of Lake County. Situated to the north of Orlando, Lake County extends for a thousand square miles in the central highlands of Florida. The word "highlands" is misleading. Towering in the flat Florida standards, the hills of Lake County are in the two hundred foot range, which causes people in Utah to chuckle. The word "lake" is not misleading, since there are more than one thousand lakes of varying circumference in the county. These lakes are part of the Ocklawaha chain. Amazingly, it is possible to travel on water in roundabout ways by lake, canal, and river, from landlocked Mount Dora to the Atlantic Ocean. Other than lakes, the county contains eighteen tiny towns spread amid grassy plains and thick patches of tropical forest. The population runs around two hundred thousand people.

Hernando de Soto, the notorious explorer, is believed to have passed through the Mount Dora vicinity in 1539. He encountered members of the Timucua tribe, who afterward disappeared from the historical record. De Soto continued westward and no one knows where the Timucua people went—it wasn't to Disney World. The first Caucasian settlers known by name in what became Mount Dora were James and Dora Ann Drawdy, who arrived from Georgia in 1846.

James Drawdy died in 1848, leaving Dora to raise their three children. She didn't stay a single mom for long. In 1849 she married James's cousin, William Drawdy. They had a number of children—the 1860 Census lists eight. William joined the Confederate Army and died in Virginia in 1862. Dora stayed a civilian and died in Florida in 1883.

Mount Dora takes its name from the lake at the southwestern border of town. Local legend suggests that *Lake* Dora was named after Dora Ann Drawdy. But this does not appear to be correct. The lake was likely named by Federal mapmakers before the Drawdys arrived. It is not known why the mapmakers chose the name *Dora*. It must be that the name meant something to one of them. We like to think the name belonged to one of the mapmaker's mothers or wives or sweethearts. We can be sure it wasn't the name of a mapmaker's *mother-in-law*—the lake wasn't polluted at that time.

The original name for what became the *town* of Mount Dora was *Royellou*. This odd concoction derived from the names of the three children—Roy, Ellen, and Lou—of Postmaster R.C. Tremain and his wife. Thankfully, the name was changed to Mount Dora in 1883—who would want to live in a place called *Royellou*? But *Mount* Dora? The highest point in town is the intersection of Lincoln Ave. and Clayton St, which is 180 feet above sea level. Visitors can reach this point without relying on ski lifts or setting up base camp on Rossiter St.

Lake Dora is approximately six miles wide and two miles long. It has an average depth of twelve feet and a maximum depth of twenty feet. Unfortunately, the water is not fit for bathing. There is considerable boating activity on the lake, however, including an active yacht club and a tour boat that makes sunset cruises. The lake is home to a large alligator population and to a number of tall bird species, including egrets, blue herons, and ibises. A colony of bald eagles nests on the southern shore; observing this colony is a highlight of the evening cruises, since the alligators dive under the surface at the first sounds of the boat's motor and become invisible. There is a small lighthouse on the lake and a nature trail in an adjoining park. The shores of the lake are ringed by expensive, if architecturally bland, homes. A number of these homes are converted houseboats.

Mount Dora was the scene of no military action in the bloody nineteenth century. The Indian wars of the early nineteenth century passed it by, as did the Civil War.

People Come from All Over to Mount Dora

Like the Drawdys, many of the early settlers came from Georgia. Among these pioneers were Dr. W. P. Henry, who named a lake for his daughter, Gertrude, and David Simpson, who staked claim to a large tract of land in town.

Georgians traveled southward in search of land. At the same time Mount Dora was also being visited by Northerners in search of a warm climate. By the 1880s the majority of families in the Mount Dora vicinity had come from the North, especially from New York and from Pennsylvania. The most important settler from the North was John Philip Donnelly, who arrived from Pittsburgh in 1879. Donnelly married a local girl, Anne Stone, whose husband had deserted her, and whose family, luckily for him, owned much of the center of town. Like many other residents, Donnelly grew oranges for a living. This was the major industry in Mount Dora until the winter of 1894-95, when a freeze killed the groves. The citrus industry didn't recover until the second half of the twentieth century.

History reports the tragic deaths in 1882 of one of the early settler families. Robert Warburton, his wife, and their two children, drowned in a place called Fiddler's Pond when their horse-and-buggy went off the road.

Mount Dora dates its official founding from 1893, when the name was changed from the awful Royellou. The town incorporated in 1910, with Donnelly as the first mayor. (Donnelly died in 1930 after a long, distinguished, and not unprofitable civic career.) The town became a city in 1953. For some odd reason unknown to healthy people, the city charter forbids the construction of a hospital within city limits. City Hall stands at the intersection of Fifth Ave. and Baker St. The present building, the second on the site, dates from 1964. The four large columns at its entrance are from the original structure.

Donnelly's large white house, an attraction in town, is a premier example of late Victorian architecture. The house is the most photographed place in Mount Dora, but it is not open to the public. It is currently the headquarters of a Masonic Lodge, so we probably don't want to know what goes on inside—the mind shudders to think of the awful rites practiced under pestle and mortar.

The house is adjacent to Donnelly Park, a tract of land Donnelly donated to the town in honor of his wife. This park has an attractive summerhouse and features in season a dazzling display of Christmas lights.

Tourism has always been an important part of the Mount Dora economy. From early in its history the town catered to wealthy Northerners, who frequently stayed for the summer. The first hotel was built on the south end of Alexander St. At Fourth Ave. and Donnelly St., a hotel stood from the 1890s well into the twentieth century. This building now houses Eduardo's Mexican Restaurant and Entertainment, a premier eating place.

One of the largest resorts was the Lakeside Inn, which by 1930 had more than one hundred rooms. Former President Calvin Coolidge and Mrs. Coolidge stayed there on a visit. "Silent Cal" became talkative when too much attention was paid to his arrival and chided the locals for interrupting his peace and quiet. We like to think "Silent Cal" avoided expletives in his eruption.

City fathers tried to induce tourism by developing an area nickname. In former years the region around Mount Dora was called "The Great Lakes of Florida" and "The Alpine Region of Florida"—the word "Alpine" really stretches it. These names did not bring in business. A slightly more successful name was "The Golden Triangle", which is the vicinity around Lakes Dora, Eustis, and Joanna.

Mount Dora Grows Steadily

Population growth in Mount Dora has always been slow. The 1900 Census listed only 197 people—and 72 African Americans. The 1920 Census reported close to eight hundred people. Between 1920 and 1950, Mount Dora had added just fifteen hundred additional people. The population peaked in the 2000 Census, with slightly more than nine thousand people.

A reason for this slow growth derives from the isolation of Mount Dora, which is located in the center of Florida away from the coasts and from any major city. It wasn't until the late nineteenth century that a rail line connected Mount Dora to the outside world. The lack of easily accessible markets prevented the development of any industry early in its history. In the twentieth century Mount Dora almost missed getting an exit on the new Route 441. This highway, which is a continuous shopping mall from one end of Florida to the other, is the major north-to-south connection. East-to-west connections are generally meandering one-lane county roads. These roads often include signs notifying drivers about "Bear Crossing".

The sparse population and geographical isolation hindered material progress in town. Electricity arrived during World War One. Incredibly, public sewerage commenced only in the Vietnam era. Air conditioning in public buildings didn't arrive until mid-century when a local bank gave its customers the chance to cool off while going broke.

There Are Black People in Mount Dora

Like many Southern towns, Mount Dora has a sad, sordid history of racial segregation. The town itself was geographically divided, with black people concentrated in the northeast section. The wealthy white folk, merchants, and tourists resided in the center of town close to the lake. The rednecks resided in the southern section, which was called "Pistolville". This does not sound like a place tourists went out of their way to visit.

The first cemetery in town was established on North Donnelly St. in 1886. The cemetery was segregated for decades, with blacks and whites idling eternity away in separate underground locations.

The first public school opened in 1881 and it, too, was segregated. Mount Dora maintained a segregated school system until the late 1960s, long after many Southern towns integrated the kudzu-draped halls of academia. Jim Crow laws remained in force until the 1960s—for example, blacks could sit only in the balcony of the local picture show.

The "Golden Triangle" region has a long history of racial violence. In 1923 members of the Klan killed a black man who had asked a white lady to dance. In 1924 a black man killed a white man who had propositioned his wife—the fate of this man must be grim. In 1928 police killed a black moonshiner.

The most notorious incident of racial violence—an incident that achieved international attention—was the Groveland Rape Case. In July, 1949, a white woman in Groveton claimed she had been attacked and raped by four black men. One of the four was killed by the posse that rounded the suspects up. The three survivors were taken into custody by Sheriff Willis V. McCall. The three were sentenced to death, but the sentence was overturned by the United States Supreme Court, which ruled that the three had not received a fair trial because jurors had seen newspaper accounts of the "confessions" and because the three had been beaten while in custody.

The situation was bad enough, but worsened on November 6, 1951, when Sheriff McCall shot two of the three suspects, killing one, while he was transporting them to another jurisdiction. McCall claimed that they were shot trying to escape. One of the surviving suspects, Walter Irwin, claimed that they were taken from the patrol car into a field and shot in cold blood. The shooting set off an international firestorm. Letters poured into Tallahassee and into the White House. The Soviet ambassador made it a *cause celebre*, saying in speeches at the United Nations that America hypocritically championed civil rights abroad while its law enforcement agents shot unarmed men in custody.

You would think that the people of Lake County would have been ashamed of Sheriff McCall's action. If not ashamed, at least concerned for their public image as a tourist destination. Unfortunately, the people of that period had a greater tolerance for shame—and the tourists didn't seem to mind, so long as the sitz stayed in the bathwater. McCall remained in office until April, 1972, despite a record of corruption, racial prejudice, and undisguised brutality. McCall saw himself as the defender of the white race against blacks and Native Americans. His deputies routinely harassed black people and accosted interracial couples who appeared in public. McCall was one of the founders of the National Association for the Advancement of White People (NAAWP). This would be funny, if people weren't being beaten and killed.

McCall was the stereotype of the hillbilly—ignorant, prejudiced, violent to the point of murder. A tall, overweight man, he personified everything that was wrong in Southern society for decades. He was Chief Bill Gillespie of *In the Heat of the Night* without the conversion. For twenty-eight years he was sheriff of Lake County. For twenty-eight years he was law and order in that place—a version of law and order.

Like many in his position, McCall eventually went too far even for po' white crackers to tolerate. He was accused of kicking to death a mentally-retarded black prisoner in April, 1972. He was tried for murder in Ocala, but was acquitted by an all-white jury. As a minimum penalty, he had to resign the position of sheriff and retire.

McCall died in 1994 at the age of eighty four. Despite his unsavory record, he remains the most famous person from Lake County. There is a road named in his honor.

A Personal Recollection

When we visited Mount Dora in December, 2003, we stopped for coffee in the Princess Antique Mall. This is a former hotel that now houses a number of concessions selling trinkets at astronomical markups. While we were sipping our lattes, a courtly gentleman of advanced years and impeccable fashion stopped by to talk. I don't recall asking, but he narrated his family history—he could trace his ancestors back centuries to the Hapsburg Empire and beyond. Somehow or other, one of his great-grandparents made it to Mount Dora. This gentleman also had some connection to the discipline of anthropology; as I recall, a friend or relative was a college professor who had written a number of books in that field. In short, he sounded like a learned man with quite a gift of gab. If his ancestors emigrated from a different part of the Old World, we could say he had quite the gift of blarney.

At the conclusion of our chat—it ended when our lattes ended—he suddenly broke into a bitter spiel about the black and brown peoples who were undermining American civilization in general and Mount Dora in particular. This turn in our conversation was immensely surprising—and it was immensely disappointing to hear such hateful speech from an old man who claimed to be a world traveler, if not in fact then in print. I would have thought his self-professed experience of the world would have bestowed a generosity of spirit and sympathy with the differently-complected peoples of the human race. Despite his connections with European royalty and with the intelligentsia of anthropology, he sounded like a racist hillbilly on Social Security.

This gentleman must be a habitué of downtown Mount Dora—I'm not sure of the effect on tourism. By chance, we caught a glimpse of him a second time on our May, 2006, visit. We were dining in a window booth in Eduardo's Mexican Restaurant and Entertainment when he strolled past, walking behind a young lady on Donnelly St. It looked as if he was doing all the talking and as if she was trying to give him the slip and failing. I'm not a lip reader, but I can make an informed guess about what the topic would turn to, if their conversation lasted long enough, which it had every appearance of doing.

The Castle

One of the most unique immigrants to Mount Dora in the early years of the twentieth century was Arthur Frothingham of Sleepy Hollow, New York. Frothingham, who was in his eighties, built The Castle, an imposing structure of eighteen rooms near the lake. None of the eighteen was a kitchen. Ever the thoughtful husband, Frothingham decided that his wife should never have to cook. They would eat out or order in, as the mood struck their fancy. Unfortunately, Frothingham died before The Castle was completed. It's not recorded whether his widow took up cooking.

After his death The Castle was inhabited for a time by Napoleon Hill, the motivational writer. (*Think and Grow Rich* was Hill's most famous work—hundreds of used copies turned up in the Barnes & Noble Sale Annex over the years, which leads me to think it was not turning out that way for the majority of readers.) The Castle was subsequently leased and rented for a number of years, but proved to be an unprofitable venture. It came down in the 1980s—the Summit Place condominiums now occupy the site where it stood. In the years of its disrepair The Castle was rumored to be haunted. No one knew for sure, but many people thought the ghost was the eccentric Frothingham.

Next Stop, China

The Castle was an imposing building that reached skyward. Mount Dora was also home to a building that reached below the ground. This was *The Catacombs*, the brain child of two resident entrepreneurs. For some reason these men became convinced that surface life on the earth was coming to an end. This belief may have stemmed from the threat of communism or from a religious fanaticism—the two were indistinguishable in the middle of the twentieth century. In any event, they commenced to build an underground bunker intended to hold twenty-five families until surface radiation dissipated. For a few thousand dollars you and your loved ones could ride out Armageddon in underground luxury. As might be predicted, their plan blew up and came to nothing—we can say their plan went south, literally. A few familial fools were separated from their money, but building on the bunker stopped for want of interest. Surface life carried on.

Impressive Changes Come to Mount Dora

The reputation of Mount Dora as a Mecca of art and antiques and its image as a redneck version of New England commenced in the 1970s. At that time a number of antique dealers moved into downtown shops, drawing collectors from near and far. Later, most of these dealers relocated out of town along Route 441. They were replaced in their turn by gift and specialty stores. One of the old hotels near the lake—the Mount Dora Hotel—was converted into the Renaissance Building that houses twenty specialty shops selling jewelry and home furnishings.

There are two bookstores on Fifth Ave. On the south side the Dickens Reed bookstore features new and used books—the selection is limited, the prices are steep. Across the street on the north side is the Old Towne bookstore; this shop sells a better selection of used books at better prices. Irish authors of some obscurity were featured in both stores—Oliver St. John Gogarty in Dillon Read and Bryan McMahon in the Old Towne. I passed on the former and purchased the latter on this visit. I suppose it will be my fate to purchase the former on the next visit. The chances are good Gogarty will be waiting on the shelf.

One of the more interesting shops in town is Uncle Al's Time Capsule on Fourth Ave. Uncle Al specializes in Hollywood memorabilia and autographs of famous people. (There is little interest in autographs of unknown people.)

We bought a *Gone with the Wind* autograph for Felicia on our first visit. I believe it was the autograph of the actress who played Scarlett's and Rhett's daughter. I bought an autograph of Victor McLaglen—how could I resist an autograph of one of the stars of *The Quiet Man*, not to mention *Gunga Din* and *The Informer*? Babci generously bought me the autograph of Billy Gilbert, a regular in Laurel and Hardy shorts, notably *The Music Box*. It's his piano the boys haul up that immense flight of stairs—and haul up and up again.

In the 1970s Mount Dora began to hold an outdoor art show in the first week in February. This annual show attracts more than twenty thousand visitors. In the 1980s an equally popular arts and crafts festival was started and Donnelly Park became a winter wonderland with a Christmas light show that summons people from across the county.

Lake Dora was prettified in 1976 during the Bicentennial celebration. A picturesque park named Simpson Cove was built at the edge of the lake. A colorful red-and-white striped lighthouse was erected in 1987. The lighthouse owns a 750-watt light and stands thirty-five feet—this is very small by lighthouse standards, but then Lake Dora is a small lake.

Adjacent to the lighthouse is Palm Island Park, which has the longest lakefront boardwalk in Florida. A bewildering number of bird species and trees can be viewed from its dung-coated planks. An alligator might slink by underneath. Excursions can be made from the boardwalk on nature trails leading inside the dank woods. Visible animal life decreases along these wet trails, but the tree specimens increase and assume unusual shapes. Oddly, some of the palm tree trunks are thicker at their peaks than at their bases. This indicated they had suffered drought in their early years—drought stunted their stumps. The trunk of one tree of unknown species had the weirdest shape. The base of this tree was knotted in such a way to resemble the emergence of a person from the wood. It literally looked as if a person—a bipedal being of some sort—was breaking through the bark. I took pictures, but they don't fully capture the uncanny appearance.

The other major industry besides tourism in the second half of the twentieth century was citrus farming, which revived in the region owing to the popularity of frozen orange juice. Lake County became a major source of orange juice for several decades. Lake County produced more than 10% of the total Florida citrus crop in the 1970s. This percentage dwindled to 2% by the end of the century, owing to several years of bad crops and rising production costs. The decline in Lake County presaged the decline of citrus production throughout Florida. Because of competition from South America, where they grow things more cheaply, and carbohydrate diets that restrict fruit consumption among chunky Americans, citrus farmers are in serious economic trouble throughout Florida. Dire forecasts suggest that within twenty years Americans will be supplied with all their orange juice from Brazil. Presumably, the citrus groves will convert to the lumber industry or be turned into strip malls, which appear to have a bright future.

Mount Dora—A Place Where Practically Nothing Ever Happened

Mount Dora is a pleasant town of mostly private houses set back on magnolia-shaded streets. Few buildings are taller than three or four stories. As advertised, the town possesses a snug quaintness that suggests New England. If the demonic summer heat isn't enough, rows of palm and citrus trees remind visitors that they are in the bottom drawer of the Confederacy. There's very little traffic in town when the festivals aren't in swing. The stores in the downtown section are homely; they open late and close early, as befits Small Town, America. There are a number of parks in town and larger state parks short drives away. The lake is picturesque, especially at dusk, when the sunsets are dramatic.

Mount Dora is a successful place, having remade itself several times—the mix of antique shops and antique people proved a winning combination. Mount Dora is also a place where people have always liked to come to, sometimes in great numbers. It is, however, a place that stands to the side of history. No battles were fought inside its borders. No armies passed through. Nothing was invented in Mount Dora. No great ideas emerged from it. No intellectual advances were made. No legends were born. No great crimes were committed on its flower-dappled sidewalks. No famous person came from there. No event of any kind has ever *put it on the map*. It is a place where practically nothing ever happened.

To say that nothing ever happened is not to disparage Mount Dora. There's something to be said for standing on the banks and not in the stream when the riptide of history is observed. War, famine, pestilence, murder, brutality, betrayal, horror, and hate—this is the record of history, even at its happiest. Who would want to be a part of that record, even by mishap or bad luck? In comparison to the dismal flow of courts and corpses, being to the side and asleep is an enviable fate. But the cash registers ring so steadily on Donnelly St., dreamless sleep is not possible.

Of course, to say that *nothing* ever happened in Mount Dora cannot be true. We would be mistaken to conflate the public with the private record. And we would be making the same mistake that O. Henry's salesman made about the hick town he visited—the dead tropical air and silence on Mount

Dora's side streets provide no hint of the mayhem breaking out behind the drapes.

A cursory review of the history of Mount Dora reveals that it is like every other place. It has stories to tell—some stories it may prefer to keep secret. Some stories are of success and of achievement, as when a young fellow from Pennsylvania arrived in town, married into wealth, and became the first citizen for decades. Some stories are of tragedies, as when an entire family disappeared into the black waters of a pond. Some stories are on the comic side, as when an old fellow from New York built a great house without a kitchen and when two loco boys went underground and made the floor the ceiling. And sometimes the stories tell of crudeness and of cruelty, as when a lawman flouted the law he was sworn to uphold. Mount Dora did not escape the racial savagery that disfigures American history. This savagery has been a theme in its story from the time of the Drawdys and I suspect the same theme is being revealed in this new century in more civilized, but no less excusable, fashion. I'm writing eight hundred miles from Donnelly St. as darkness pours across the East Coast. I'm confident a well-dressed elderly gentleman is on the prowl looking to bend someone's ear with his particular explanation of Mount Dora's social woes.

I have a feeling that if we stayed in town for more than a few days, we might find out more than we cared to know.

THE AMBER COUNTRY
JESCE RAZ

Lithuania—June, 2007

May 31

Ten years after our first visit Babci and I returned to Lithuania *jesce raz*—that's Polish for "again" and pronounced *yester raz*. On this trip we were accompanied by Luke Ford, then aged thirteen. Luke was, in fact, the purpose of the trip. There is little genealogical information left among our cousins in The Amber Country. Researching Lithuanian family history amounts to waiting—and waiting and waiting—for responses from the Vilnius Archive. We had teased Luke so often about *Lithe-uania* that it was time to take him there. It was especially important to Babci that Luke visit the ancestral homeland with her.

We left Newark Airport on Scandinavian Airlines flight 9662 on May 30 at 5:50 PM. We arrived in Copenhagen at 9:35 AM on May 31. We made connections with Air Baltic flight 162 and arrived in Vilnius around noon.

I don't know how it was for Babci or for Luke, but the flight was the easiest I ever made on a Trans-Atlantic jaunt. I had an aisle seat, the plane was half empty, and I took a melatonin tablet, which induced the most relaxing sleep. Four shots of cognac contributed to delivering a safe landing in the airport of paradoxical sleep.

The calmness and contentment inspired by chemistry changed on the instant to neuronal inflammation when we learned on arrival that our baggage hadn't accompanied us. We spent the day worrying that we would have to spend the next day buying clothing rather than touring. I was instructed to call the airport at midnight—they assumed the luggage was put on the next plane. We must be good people living a good life—to our immense relief the bags arrived at the hotel a half hour before I tried conversing over the phone with people who didn't comprehend English.

In Vilnius we stayed at the Hotel Scandic Neringa located on Gedimino *Gatve*. This is a first-class hotel run by Scandinavians, which means things were efficient and clean. The only odd thing was the lack of soap. I should say lack of *bars* of soap. For some ecological reason I didn't understand, soap was available only in liquid form.

The hotel is connected with a pizzeria and has an upscale dining room. We ate continental breakfasts in the dining room during our stay.

I think I got the better room. My room faced the inside. Luke and Babci's room faced Gedimino *Gatve*. The hotel is across the street from a night club, so every time a patron entered or left, their paradoxical sleep got obliterated with deafening blasts of rock music.

I misunderstood the location of the Scandic. I thought it was to the east of McDonald's and closer to the Cathedral. In fact, the hotel was to the west, closer to KGB headquarters and to Lukiskiu Square—this is the park where the colossal statue of Lenin stood in the communist period. (There are famous photographs of the statue being torn down and lopped apart limb-by-limb when democracy was achieved.) I had an odd memory experience when Luke and I took a walk. I remembered there was a park between Gedimino *Gatve* and the Green Bridge, so we happily traipsed through Lukiskiu arriving at the Neris River one bridge to the west. It didn't disturb me that the Square was devoid of trees and shrubbery—it's just flat open space and as bald as Lenin was. Only on our return was I able to orient myself and find the right way back.

It was a moving experience to return to Snipiskiu *Gatve*. The Hotel Naujasis Vilnius is still there, as is the immense Lietuva. Snipiskiu is built up with a row of stores I did not recollect—the area has become a shopping district. The streets were as congested as I remembered, since a number of buses and trolleys converge in front of St. Raphael's. It was also moving to cross the Green Bridge again. A bridge has been in this location since the sixteenth century. The present bridge dates to 1952. Ponderous bronze statues representing Youth, Agriculture, Industry, and Peace remain at the entrances of the bridge from the communist years. They haven't been razed, as the people have grown fond of them. I'm sure many of the thousands who pass below the statues give a sly wave or salute as they say, "Good morning," or "Good evening," as the case might be. I wasn't embarrassed to wave to Industry and Peace as I offered an enthusiastic "Good afternoon, my bronze friends!"

In the afternoon the three of us strolled the Old Town. It was grand to see the familiar sights. The Cathedral and Castle Hill, the bell tower still keeping time, Pilies *Gatve* with its procession of churches, the Church of St. Anne's and, still standing watch behind it, the wonderful Church of the Bernardines. The streets of the Old Town were crowded with tourists. The faces of the buildings were in much greater repair than in our previous visit. Many buildings had outdoor cafes. The street at the lower end of Pilies— nearer the Dawn Gate—was under repair, which made it difficult for Babci to proceed. The street was so torn up, we could have been in New Jersey.

When we returned to the Scandic we found Mecislav Bielawski and his family waiting. They presented us with flowers and with candy. When we last met Mecislav, he was engaged to be married. He has two children now, Gretta and Ernest, both of whom were shy and on the verge of tears, hiding behind their parents. I bent over, smiled, and told them, "We're Americans, you don't have to be scared," but that didn't work.

Later that evening we met Gintautas Pupalaigis, his sister Irena, and Marija, their mother. (Marija is the daughter of Juzufa Kozlowska, who we had the honor of meeting in 2000. Juzufa passed away, aged ninety one, in 2002.) Seven of us squeezed into a compact car meant for four and drove to a scenic park at the outskirts of Vilnius. We dined there and strolled the grounds of the park, which is situated atop a hill overlooking the Neris River. At this location the Neris rushes along wearing whitecaps, unlike its motionless passage below the Green Bridge. The park, which is used for concerts, had a rustic, somewhat rugged, quality.

Communication was easy, since Gintautas, who works as a customs supervisor, speaks English. We spoke about general topics—the world situation, the Lithuanian and American economies, and a smattering of family history.

June 1

We renewed our friendship with the sights of the Old Town, although we didn't proceed farther on Pilies than to the Town Hall, which is about halfway from the Cathedral. Babci and Luke waited, while I ran on ahead looking for the Cognac Boutique, advertised in *Vilnius in Your Pocket* as being at Number Four Etmony *Gatve*. I found Number Four Etmony *Gatve*, but it was a private dwelling. There was no boutique in sight, still less one that sold cognac out of oak casks. Maybe I needed to know the secret knock.

We weren't able to locate the *miracle tile* that is on the pavement somewhere in front of the Cathedral. This tile marks the spot where the two-million-member chain of people commenced to protest communism in 1989. Finding it is supposed to bring good luck. (The other *miracle tile* is located in Tallinn, Estonia, where the chain concluded.) I think you're supposed to stand on the tile and spin around, which is sillier than waving to the statues on the Green Bridge. We waited and watched, but no one spun, so we were clueless.

One of the emotional highlights of the trip was taking a picture of Babci and Luke in the same place I photographed Babci in 1997. This is in a corner of the red-brick gate that leads from St. Anne's to the Church of the Bernardines. We don't need to spin on tiles or engage in superstitious stunts—the years have been very kind that we were able to return to this exact place a full decade after our initial visit.

That evening, we met Mecislav and his family and our Storta cousin Wladyslawa Kucsynska for dinner. The evening started out with considerable confusion as we thought Mecislav and his wife were taking us to a local restaurant they knew. Turned out the place was a self-service restaurant that would have been inappropriate for a family gathering. We retraced our steps and dined in the Scandic Neringa instead. It was difficult to make conversation with so many people. Mecislav and his family do not speak a word of English; nor does Wladyslawa. Babci doesn't speak much Polish at this stage, but she was able to serve as an able translator. We limited our statements to single clauses, so we got by. There were a lot of confused looks as Babci translated—I'm sure Luke and I looked as confused—followed by nods and *taks* as the meaning got across. (*Tak* is Polish for "yes"—it's pronounced *tak*.) If the meaning didn't get across, we never knew it.

I'm happy to report that Gretta and Ernest warmed to us after a while. "See, Americans aren't bad people." I think the bowls of ice cream and chocolate syrup helped persuade them.

June 2

We were picked up promptly at 9:00 AM for the three-hour drive across Lithuania to Klaipeda. The highway was in fine repair, the traffic was light, and there wasn't a toll booth in sight—we knew weren't in New Jersey. The drive was uneventful, the scenery bland. The land is flat and mostly reserved for cattle. I didn't see much cultivation of crops—and I didn't see many cows, at that. There wasn't much industry along the highway and not a single strip mall or billboard.

Klaipeda is a huge sprawling seaport located on the Baltic coast in a region historically referred to as Lithuania Minor. The current population is 187,000. This was a heavily Germanic section until World War Two, when the Germans fled to be replaced by Lithuanians and Soviets.

We met our guide, Emilia A—, a middle-aged lady of great knowledge and ethnic pride. Emilia was very proud of Lithuania and very opposed to communism and to Russia. When we told her that we had toured Salcininki on our former visit, Emilia disparaged the Slavs in southeastern Lithuania as being slothful and unpatriotic. I think she misunderstood our ancestry. She must have thought we were Balts—people of our quality couldn't possibly be descended from those awful Slavs.

Emilia's inadvertent habit of disparaging our ancestry can be called an *overslight*. She didn't mean to, and we didn't take it personally.

Emilia expounded on history while were standing near Theater Square— this is a parking lot behind a theater. On March 22, 1939, Adolf Hitler gave a speech from the balcony we faced. Hitler gave an ultimatum—we might call it an *ulterromatim* to the Lithuanian leadership that Klaipeda be returned to the Reich. I never read the speech, but we can be fairly certain that *Der Fuhrer* disparaged the Slavs to the benefit of the Balts, who are related to the Prussians, which makes them okay.

Klaipeda was the border between East Prussia and Lithuania for centuries. The city was originally called Memel, the region Memelburg. This made residents "Memelburgers" or "Memel Landers", phrases which led to incessant merriment between Luke and me, as in the question we wore out, "How are things in Memel Land?"

Memel was invaded and annexed by Lithuania in 1923. (Lithuania had been a province of Russia for a century; it became a sovereign state for a few years between the World Wars.) The name was changed from Memel to Klaipeda, which is Lithuanian for "marsh". It was in Nazi hands from 1941 to 1945, when the Soviet Army captured the city after fierce fighting. This is a region that saw heavy destruction in World War Two. Entire sections of the city needed to be rebuilt following the war. Emilia pointed out that many small parks were created from vacant lots of bombed buildings.

As they did with other "liberated" nations, the Soviets ravaged the territory and left stupefaction behind. We toured the "Blacksmith's Museum", which was created by a man named Dionizas Varkalis to salvage iron crosses and weathervanes stolen from churches and cemeteries. The impetus for this kind of depository came from a scandalous episode in 1977 when the Soviets decided to convert a cemetery into a city park. Drunken laborers were put to work tearing down monuments and tombstones. We passed the park on the drive to Palanga. It now holds a number of abstract sculptures and is in an upscale section of the city. I'm not sure I'd want children to dig in the sandbox.

After our tour of Klaipeda we were driven to Palanga, which is about a half hour to the north on a major road. On the way we passed the only functioning oil derrick in Lithuania.

Located on the Baltic, Palanga is the chief Lithuanian resort. The city is near the Germanized "Little Lithuania", but has always been associated with Lithuania. The tour book advised that it was a crowded and rowdy place, but we found the opposite to be true. It was quiet and peaceful and the side streets were mostly devoid of pedestrians. But then we weren't outside at two in the morning.

The vicinity has been occupied by humans for thousands of years. The first occurrence in the historical record was in 1161 when King Valdemar of Denmark landed in a campaign against the Curonian tribes. In the intervening centuries Palanga has been the site of battles and ravages engaged in by assorted invaders—Teutonic Knights, Livonians, Swedes, and, of course, the Germans and Russians. The Polish Count Michael Tyszkiewicz purchased Palanga in 1824. Descendants built the palace that now houses the Amber Museum.

Palanga is associated with the legend of Birute (died 1382), wife of Kestutis, Grand Duke of Lithuania. Birute was a priestess devoted to virginity. Overcome by lust, Kestutis raped her—actually, he raped her six times, since history records they had six children. Kestutis was defeated in battle and murdered by his nephew—family values were less strong in those days. Birute fled Lithuania and afterward drowned, although it is not clear where. One legend claims she died in Palanga, where a pagan cult formed in her memory. Another legend claims she died in Poland. Supposedly, she is buried on a hill on the coast in Palanga.

We were a long way from the United States, but I was completely at home. I sat with Luke in the Hotel Palangos Vetra, sipping brandy, eating pistachio nuts— and watching *professional wrestling*, the universal sport. At 10:00 PM on June 2 in Palanga, Lithuania, on what sounded like a Russian-language station—number seven on the dial—we watched Ric Flair, the immortal "Nature Boy" and sixteen-time world champion, get double-crossed by his "protégé", Carlito. The announcers spoke in English, as they do on *Monday Night Raw* on the USA network. There was additional commentary by a Russian who screamed voice-over the Americans.

It sounded a bit odd to hear two languages simultaneously, but I suppose it really didn't matter what anyone was screaming, since this was professional wrestling.

June 3

The Hotel Palangos Vetra is a small and attractive place of twenty-nine rooms located on Daukanto *Gatve* across the street from the Botanical Garden. Babci and Luke were on the second floor, I was on the third. I definitely had the better accommodations. My room was spacious with windows that opened to the west and ran across the entire wall.

The interior of the hotel was unusual. A glass atrium led to hallways where the rooms were located. To conserve energy, the corridors were dark. I had to tap a panel on the wall to light the path to see my way to the room. As the light stayed on for only a few seconds, I had to step quickly.

Like the Scandic Neringa in Vilnius, the Palangos Vetra had that odd aversion to bars of soap. It's not easy to shave or to wash your hair with liquid soap.

The hotel had a decent continental breakfast. It also had the worst coffee I have ever tasted. I would say it was the worst coffee in the world, but I haven't been everyplace—still, I can't imagine coffee any worst than what they served. It was like drinking pencil shavings—I apologize to the shavings. The fifty-cent coffee in the machine in Hutchinson Hall in Kean University tasted like the richest latte in comparison.

Emilia arrived at 10:00 AM to take us on a tour of what is grandiloquently referred to as the "Botanical Garden". In fact, the Garden was little more than a forested park. The only landscaped sections were the grounds near the Amber Museum. The tour book brags that the Garden was an artificially created "wilderness," but it really wasn't. I suppose it's what city managers and naturalists believed Palanga looked like before human beings arrived to spoil everything.

Emilia led us through the park to the Tyszkiewicz Palace—now the Amber Museum. The Palace is exactly what is seen in movies—maybe I saw this one in a movie. It's a large imposing building of several stories, intimidatingly rectangular, and with double staircases that curve steeply upward. Looking down from the oversized door, I felt like the lord of the manor. Looking up at the house from ground level, I felt like what I was supposed to feel like—a peasant.

The Amber Museum was founded in 1963. There are now more than twenty-five thousand pieces of amber laid out in magnified display cases in what had been private rooms and apartments. The amber is laid out according to type and inclusion. The latter can include insects, spiders, leaves, and soil, all captured in pine resin millions of years ago. We were able to peruse the amber at our leisure for a while, but the narrow rooms soon became as crowded as a trolley car in Vilnius when a tour group of pushy foreigners arrived.

Amber is *gintaro* in Lithuanian. I like the word *amber* more than I like the word *gintaro.*

I bought a small piece of amber with an embedded insect. As we parted for the day, Emilia claimed I paid too much. I don't know whether that's true and I have to defer to her judgment. I do know that the price of amber has increased since our first visit ten years ago. The finest piece I own, with an insect visible even to people with macular deficiencies, cost a fraction of what I paid at the museum gift shop.

The Palangos Ventra is four long residential blocks from the main drag, Basanaviciaus *Gatve.* The houses are large and set back from the street. There are a lot of trees and shrubbery on the path. Except for tourists headed for the attractions, no one seemed to be about. Traffic was light. The sidewalks are broken up and pebbly, so we had to be careful to keep Babci on level ground. By the end of our visit, we were well-trained pedestrians. We knew precisely what sections to avoid and when to cross the street.

Basanaviciaus is the Baltic version of an American boardwalk, except that it's a street. It's closed off to traffic in places, but open in others, so you have to stay on the ball else you tour the attractions in the other world.

One of the unusual sights on Basanaviciaus was the presence of Segways and small motorized scooters. Despite being touted as the invention that would change the world, Segways never caught on in the United States. I'm not sure why—it could be the price, it could the issue of self-esteem—but they seem to have caught on in Palanga. Everyone from dressed-down teens to middle-aged businessmen in suits whizzed by on them. Scooters were mostly limited to dressed-down teens. Regardless who drove them, scooters tended to zip by at excessive rates of speed. They could easily send you to the local hospital where you could express the accent-free language of pain.

A right turn at the intersection of Daukanto and Basanaviciaus led to the Church of the Assumption, which is a large red-brick building celebrating its hundredth birthday. (*Sto Lat!* This is Polish for "one hundred years" and pronounced *sto lat.*) There were vendors outside the church gates selling trinkets and pieces of amber. A short walk of two blocks from the church led to what must be an innovation in this region of Lithuania—a supermarket on the grand scale of an American Acme or Shop Rite. I ventured inside one time and bought some snacks for the hotel and the requisite bottle of brandy. They charge extra for the bags.

Emilia made disparaging remarks about the supermarket. She fears the inevitable. Such a convenient store will put small vendors out of business. Emilia prefers local product and a small scale. As we saw in Salcininki, the people in Palanga keep vegetable gardens outside the city where they are able to grow their own produce. I suppose Emilia fears that the supermarket will cause the collapse of this quaint system of homegrown produce. There will be no need to tend to gardens when the people can go to the supermarket and buy the same items they break their backs to grow. Vestiges of peasantry will collapse altogether.

In the other direction Basanaviciaus *Gatve* leads to the Baltic Sea. There are few stores in this direction and one amusement ride, a bizarre contraption that twisted round and upside down in every direction except inside out. I got motion sickness merely looking at the ride. A crowd of people stood in front and watched as hardy souls experimented with gravity. A hawker screamed in Lithuanian, challenging people to come on board and lose the contents of their stomachs.

The rest of Basanaviciaus was quiet and sedate, consisting of a continuous series of restaurants and bars, all with outdoor seating. As we found in Vilnius, the menus are astonishingly large. I don't see how they can prepare everything that's advertised—maybe it's the same dish in other words. Most of the menus include English descriptions, which is fortunate, since the servers do not speak English. Despite the cosmopolitan nature of Palanga, the servers aren't up to the standards of the servers in Vilnius. They don't appear to be as fully trained. They have a disquieting habit of presenting fifteen-page menus and then standing and waiting for the orders, pencils and notepads in hand. This doesn't work, unless you happen to be a polyglot speed-reader. I was usually able to buy some time by requesting a glass of *alus*, one word in Lithuanian I pronounced correctly.

Basanaviciaus rises steeply near the shoreline and then descends gently, concluding in a small park at the edge of the beach. Rows of benches allow visitors to sit and ponder the verities as they stare into the Baltic Sea. But this is not the place for quiet contemplation. The place is crowded, street musicians compete for contributions, small children run about, adults converse in a farrago of languages, and grown men whiz by on odd-shaped contraptions.

Seeing the Baltic Sea—*Baltijos Jura* in Lithuanian—was a moving experience. I felt like a child brought to the ocean for the first time. The sea looked exactly like I had expected. The water was seriously gray and slightly darker than the gray sky. The sun was a dull splotch that threw no reflection on the surface of the water. Luke and I kicked our sneakers off and descended to the beach that laid below a wall of dunes covered with scraggly maritime shrubs and trees. The beach was about a third the width of the beach at

Wildwood Crest, which sets the standard. I wasn't thinking right or I would have brought along a container in which to scoop sand for the windowsill.

The water was very cold—I had expected this. We walked in up to the knees and no higher. No one was swimming, although every now and then young men ran out about thirty or forty yards and then circled back to the shore. I'm not sure what this practice was about, but I suspect it may have involved a dare. Maybe it involved a tease. It certainly involved second thoughts. Fortunately for them, the water was shallow.

There were a few people strolling in the low water. Probably, they were tourists. There was a rather rough soccer game in progress. The players—combatants, I should say—were of diverse ages and physical conditions. A few were obviously muscular types. Others were what William Sheldon, a mid-twentieth century psychologist, called "endomorphs". Civilians use the word "fat". The most out-of-shape players wore the skimpiest bathing trunks. There must be a negative correlation between the overhang of a person's paunch and the skimpiness of that person's bathing trunks. If William Sheldon were alive, he would consider this a worthy conjecture to test.

As we walked I kept my eyes peeled to the wrack with the hope that I might spot a piece of amber in the raw. Unfortunately, I came up empty-eyed. Residents say the only time amber drifts ashore is after a storm. The day we visited, the sea was quiet, more lacustrine than oceanic. The beach face was devoid of shells, seaweed, and specimens. It was the cleanest wrack I've even seen, which is what we would expect of a people related to the Prussians.

Luke and I strolled into the grayness on the long pier that commences at the foot of Basanaviciaus *Gatve*. There's been a pier at this site for years. The present one dates to 1998, when it replaced a pier broken up in a storm. The pier proceeds a good distance from the beach and makes a dramatic turn to the right. I don't recall anyone fishing from the pier, which was used for walking, sight-seeing, and photography. There's a custom in Palanga that people come to the pier at twilight—in summer this means 11:00 PM—and wave good-by to the sun. They also remind the sun not to forget to come back the next morning.

June 4

Today we drove back to Klaipeda and toured the Curonian Spit. This is a narrow peninsula of sand and maritime forest that runs to the south from Klaipeda to the Kaliningrad region of Russia. The Spit does not connect with the city of Klaipeda but must be reached by ferry.

The Spit separates the Baltic Sea from an inland body of water called the Curonian Lagoon. The word "lagoon" isn't understood in the American sense of lush blue tropical ponds, like they show in movies. Instead, the Lagoon is as gray as the Baltic—I'm sure it is as cold. As we proceeded to the west, the Lagoon becomes so wide the opposite shore is no longer visible.

There is a single road in good repair that runs all the way to the Russian border. The peninsula is now heavily forested—reforestation began in the nineteenth century when the primeval forest was stripped for housing and for fuel. In earlier times the loss of forest caused the loss of sand, since the tree trunks shielded the sand from blowing away and the roots tied everything is place. Literally, the Spit is a beach and beaches have a way of altering themselves in the winds and floods.

Our first stop was the village of Juodkrante, which translates as "black shore". The village was first mentioned in 1429, but underwent a number of restorations over the centuries. The village disappeared entirely in the seventeenth century only to slowly recover into our own time. In the nineteenth century Juodkrante became a tourist attraction and a center of amber harvesting.

In 1979 local artisans carved oversized wood sculptures of Biblical figures and Lithuanian folk characters on the "Hill of Witches". Babci stayed behind with our driver in the tourist depot and Luke, Emilia, and I toured the hill. The sculptures are a delight to see—some are interactive, meaning you can push and climb on them. However, the path is unpaved and rutted. You have to spend as much time watching the ground as the figures.

We came on a group of high school students visiting the hill. Emilia took hold of a blond girl and started to sing a folk song. She invited us to join hands and dance around in an impromptu quickstep. It was completely unchoreographed and chaotic, but a lot of fun. It was like a Lithuanian version of "ring around the rosie".

We pulled to the side of the road west of Juodkrante and climbed a tower to view the flocks of herons and cormorants that nest in the trees. There are more than five hundred of the former and two thousand of the latter, none of them paying rent. The cormorants express ghastly high-pitched howls— imagine the sound of laughing gulls pitched ten times higher. Their droppings are destroying this section of forest, but they are a protected species in the European Union, so nothing can be done.

After a stop at a high-end amber gallery, where we bankrupted ourselves buying specimens with and without insect inclusions, we proceeded to the village of Nida, population two thousand. This is the Bowling Green in this part of Lithuania. The rest of the Spit belongs to Russia.

Nida is a picturesque place. Part of it is a reconstructed "fisherman's village" of quaint thatched cottages and enclosed gardens. There has been a village called Nida on or near here since the fifteenth century and probably for long before that. The village is on its current site since 1794.

There are Lithuanian folk tales about forests and lakes that get up and move of their own accord. I don't know if that is possible—I tend to think not—but villages on the Spit do wander from place to place, owing to the drift of the sand. In New Jersey we call this "shoredrift", a word I consider the most beautiful in the English language. (I used to think "peachblown" was the most beautiful word; it is now in second place. The personal name "Melissa" is in third place. In fourth place—I better stop at third place, as this can go on indefinitely.) Decades of wind and storms can cause changes in the structure of a peninsula built of sand. Loss of trees accelerates the process.

The new forest shields the sand—the forest also hides the scars of battle. The Spit was the site of brutal fighting at the end of World War Two.

Nida was associated with East Prussia and with Germany—as the war ended the Germans went west to return as tourists in our time. Nida is strongly associated with the writer Thomas Mann who resided in a cabin at the edge of the Lagoon—Mann lived in Nida for only a few years, so it's a stretch to claim him as a favorite son. In communist times Nida was reserved for the *nomenklatura* and could be visited by invitation only. The area was off limits to the hoi polloi, so was preserved and kept unspoiled.

We had a delightful lunch in Nida at an outdoors café. We talked politics and religion with Emilia, who disclosed that she did not own a television set. Instead of watching the boob tube, she reads, writes, and prays, all of which are to her credit.

Our last stop in Nida was to stroll the edge of the very white and very tall dunes that mark the end of town. Some of these dunes rise five stories over sea level. The appearance of the dunes was like a desert, and it may well have been one, as the heat was intense—it was a foretaste of what I'll experience in eternity. We could see Russia across the dunes. I would have tried to collect sand at this place, but there were too many eyes on me. The attempt to sift sand into my empty water bottle may have triggered an international incident.

We drove back to Palanga and took our leave of Emilia, who had been an informed and gracious guide to a part of the world we shall unlikely see again. That evening, we strolled the long blocks to Basanavicius *Gatve* for the last time—for the record the names of the streets are, in order, Kestucio, Dz. Simsono, and A. Mickevicius. We dined at one of the outdoors restaurants near the church. I selected a delicious creamy mushroom dish from a menu as wide as a chapter book.

As we returned to the hotel I wondered what the native Palangans thought of us. We must have looked liked tourists—yet, there were so many people wandering about, we might have passed as locals provided we kept our mouths closed. We tend to be lean people, which put us in the Balt camp. A running joke we had is that you can tell where people are from by their physiques. Germans and Slavs tend to be on the circular side, Balts on the rectangular side, and Americans in between—all right, Americans are generally circular people, although not as circular as the Germans and the Slavs.

On June 5 we left Palanga at 7:00 AM on Scandinavian Airlines flight 2749 to Copenhagen. There was a layover in Copenhagen of several hours, time enough to empty our wallets in the duty-free shop. I don't know what Luke and Babci bought. I know I bought cognac and licorice—I always buy cognac and licorice in these places. The connecting flight was number 909 to Newark, where we arrived at 2:45 PM. Our travels were over. The Amber Country was left behind for a third time. Twice before I thought I'd never see *Lietuva* again, so I didn't make this claim when we landed in Newark. I was wrong in 1997 and I was wrong in 2000. It took a few years, but we returned to Lithuania. All the knowledge and wisdom in the world are no help in predicting the trips that await in the future. I'll stay quiet and resist the urge to be wrong a third time.

Printed in the United States
By Bookmasters